Purls of

Wisdom

Don Hansler

Purls of Wisdom © 1995
By Donald D. Hansler

Publisher's Cataloging in Publication

Hansler, Don.
    Purls of wisdom: 94 three-minute moments of unconventional
views to fill life's short breaks / Don Hansler.
    p. cm.
    Preassigned LCCN: 95-60178.
    ISBN: 1-886839-12-3

    1. Essays.   I. Title.
PS3558.A5675P87 1995   814'.54

                              QBI95-223

Published by:
    Fun Ed. Productions
    22711 66th Avenue, Court East
    Spanaway, WA 98387
Production by:
    Frontier Publishing
    Seaside, OR 97138

Preface

If you have lived a full life, you could hardly have escaped hearing the phrase, "Pearls of Wisdom." Perhaps when you first saw the title of this book you thought the word *Purls* was misspelled.

No, that is not the case. A *purl* is a stitch in the knitting process. It is an alternative to the knit stitch. If you want your knitted fabric to have a consistent, unchanging texture, you use only the knit stitch. But if you want to add variety and texture to your fabric, you may use the purl stitch.

As you read this book, you will find that most of the articles present unconventional viewpoints on the topics at hand. I hope these articles will add variety and texture to the fabric of your life,

That is why I call them *purls*.

Don Hansler

Table of Contents

About the Author

By all standards, the author, Don Hansler, is a "Senior Citizen." He grew up during the Great Depression. He barely missed the draft during World War II but did serve in the U.S. Army during the Korean War.

Hansler finished high school, college, and graduate school, then pursued and successfully completed a 32-year career in the field of education.

During that career, he worked with the full spectrum of students, from kindergarten to college graduate level.

He and his wife, Marge, raised three children to adulthood.

The lifetime of experiences that led to his current Senior Citizen status demonstrated to him that there is usually more than one way to interpret almost any event, situation, problem or phenomenon. This book, entitled *Purls of Wisdom* reflects that conclusion.

As you read this book, you will be exposed to many essays that express unconventional points of view, ways of looking at events, situations, problems and phenomena that are different from what can be called "conventional wisdom."

The author is convinced it will take unconventional, and in some cases radical, approaches to interpreting and dealing with human behavior if our species is to avoid self-destruction and to maximize quality of life.

Read — sometimes with amusement, sometimes with astonishment, sometimes with concern — what he has written in this series of easy-to-read essays.

Purls of

Wisdom

Don Hansler

The Drip-bucket Phenomenon

B ack in the good old days, the economy of the country of Remacia was humming along, boosted mainly by its two main wood-products industries: making wooden shingles for roofs, and making wooden drip-buckets to place under leaks in roofs. Now, they had a real good thing going, because every home needed a roof, and the wooden shingles were the best roofing materials available. But, shingle roofs only lasted without leaking for about five years, and then the homeowner had to start buying drip-buckets to place under each leak as it appeared. Drip-bucket sales gradually outpaced shingle sales. As a result, a lot of Remacian entrepreneurs started new businesses based on newly invented versions of the wooden drip buckets.

But then a frightful thing happened: the country of Napaj introduced a plastic drip bucket. Well you can imagine what happened to the stocks of the Remacian wooden drip-bucket companies. They plunged almost overnight as thousands of investors panicked, and many people lost their entire life savings because of the crash. The swifter and wiser of the investors sold their stocks before the crash gained momentum, and they later wisely reinvested their funds in Napajese drip-buckets.

While hundreds of Remacian wooden drip-bucket companies were going bankrupt, equal numbers of Napajese companies were starting up and making a

2

killing in the drip-bucket market by exporting their products to Remacia. As time went by, the very resourceful and creative Napajese rapidly invented improved models of the original plastic bucket, and numerous small Napajese companies that were based upon the manufacture and sales of these new models began operations. They greatly stimulated the Napajese economy by hiring thousands of Napajese workers for their manufacturing plants.

Well, the Remacians, who have always been known as survivors in times of turmoil, gradually re-geared their wooden drip-bucket factories so that they could manufacture copies of the Napajese plastic drip-buckets. Before very long, the Remacian economy began to recover because of the newly retrieved drip-bucket sales. The highly superior scientific and technological skills of the Remacians even permitted them to develop plastic drip-buckets that surpassed the quality of the Napajese ones. It wasn't very long before the Remacians and Napajese were blissfully sharing and co-dominating the world drip-bucket market.

However, one day panic gripped the Napajese and Remacian financial markets. It all arose because of a headline article in the country of Mergany's leading fiscal newspaper. The headline read as follows: "Mergan Inventor Introduces New Permanent Roofing Material."

Ever since then, the term "drip-bucket" has been used to describe any effort that is aimed at solving a peripheral problem rather than the basic underlying problem.

Efficiency

The quickest way isn't necessarily the fastest way. A task approached with excessive haste is often foiled by counterproductive complications. A case in point is the process of untying your shoelaces. Have you ever noticed that when you try to speed up that procedure, you usually end up with a knot more challenging than the Gordian variety. Of course, when you're in a big hurry, the inclination to take the slow, sure way with your shoelaces is overwhelmed by the inherent appeal of gambling with a faster approach; no matter that years of disastrous experience with that gamble have indicated near certainty of failure.

Another example of false temporal economy is the instinct that tells one to carry more grocery bags from the store to the car than is humanly possible. That proclivity knows no bounds of race, age, or sex. To observe the truth of the latter statement, just park sometime where you can observe shoppers coming out of a grocery store. Of course, the instinct applies equally well to the process of carrying the groceries from the car to the house, too. Inveterate excess-grocery carriers often find themselves with broken bottles of anything from applesauce to zucchini all over the garage floor. But the memory of the post-gamble cleanup appears not to linger long enough in the minds of most shoppers to prevent a similar set-back on future shopping trips.

Probably the classic example of misdirected time-saving measures is that of speeders trying to get to their destination faster than the law will allow. Most of us have tangled with that temptation a time or two. Well, the good news is that our traffic fines go to a good cause - that of supporting local government. The elimination of the speeding ticket would probably result in the need for a significant increase in local taxes. We can thank roadway gamblers for keeping our tax rates at a level no higher than they already are.

My last example of time-saving myths is the too hastily zipped zipper. What male among you can honestly say that he has never caught his shirttail in the zipper of his fly because of excessive haste. And, I'll bet that not many of you females can truthfully tell me that you have never snagged your slip in the zipper of your dress because you were trying to make up for lost time.

So, the next time you're tempted to gamble on a high-risk time-saving technique, remember what wise men have known down through the ages: the quickest way isn't necessarily the fastest way.

Managing Our Money

Y ou shouldn't manage your money in such a way that your spouse would be financially better off with you dead! That advice may seem self-evident to some readers, but most of the *men* that I know are not heeding it. Most of my male acquaintances have so much life insurance on themselves that I'm surprised they still allow their wives to prepare their food. I want my wife and kids to *miss* me when I'm gone, especially my wife. A lot of the married women that I know would have reason to be justifiably delighted to find out that their spouses had kicked the bucket.

I have a friend who lives in Las Vegas, and he reports that droves of rich widows descend upon that resort town every week, eager to enjoy spending the riches that their departed spouses have left behind. In talking to many of those rich widows, he discovers that many of them had husbands who were downright skinflints during most of their wedded life, and who rarely allowed them to spend money on anything that could be even loosely interpreted to be a luxury item. And now that their misers are gone, they're in Vegas living it up and making up for lost time.

I have a friend in his 70s who has played miser to his wife for all of their nearly half-century of marriage. Unfortunately for her, she may be too old to enjoy the old guy's money by the time that he reaches his demise. She never gets to spend a penny without a major document of justification. From conversations with her about their net worth, I conclude that she would be about 3.2 times better off financially with him dead. Now, if you ask me, that's just too much temptation to add a little lethal additive to the morning coffee. I have never been able to figure out why his type of guy doesn't wake up to reality and live it up a little while both he and his wife are still *alive*. If they were near poverty, I wouldn't be so critical, but they have a net worth that would take years for his widow to spend, even if she went on a wild shopping spree every day of the week.

Although all of the discussion to this point has centered on the assumption that the male member of the married duo has the more miserly inclinations, the reverse of all of those statements would pretty well hold if the situation were reversed. However, the actuarial statistics indicate that there is a significantly greater chance that a woman will outlive her husband, rather than the other way around. That may be because men expend so much energy having fun, like golfing, hunting, and fishing. Maybe our Maker intended that men have more fun while the couple are both alive, and women have more fun after one of them is dead.

There's No Free Lunch

Some people will give just about anything to get something for nothing! Astute advertisers have known that fact for a long time. Just put the word "FREE" on the outside of a bulk advertising mailing, and it is just about certain to be opened and read by millions who would normally otherwise assign such pieces to the junk mail circular file.

One thing that the astute *consumer* learns, however, is that the large word "FREE" on any advertising is almost always accompanied by extensive amounts of fine print which disclose that the free item has more strings attached to it than a puppet octopus.

One ad that I saw from this category was displayed by an automobile dealership. The dealer's readerboard said, in large print that was readable from several blocks away, "Free Radar Detector." Any potential customer who was lured by that sign could discover quickly, by reading the fine print that was available in the dealer's showroom, that all you had to do to get the "Free" radar detector was to purchase one of their $68,000, 120 mile-per-hour luxury automobiles. That's some fine print, I'd say.

All that you have to do to get *some* of the free gifts is to fill out a name and address card. However, most gullible consumers haven't yet learned that that one card can result in several hundred pounds of junk mail advertising being delivered to your address. By filling out such a card, you're practically signing away

8

your right to privacy for the rest of your life, but that thought doesn't deter the zealous pursuer of things that are "Free."

Before I learned the reality of "free" gift offerings, I fell prey to an ad about "free" sleeping bags for those who would simply drop by and look at the offerings of a local camping club. Of course, the "drop by" involved about a three-hour drive each way for me and my family. Well, since we wanted to take a drive anyway on that pleasant Sunday afternoon, I figured that the investment in the driving expense and time was warranted by the opportunity to get the free sleeping bag. When we arrived at the camping club, we discovered that you had to sign up for a three-hour tour. Well, I decided to endure the tour for the sake of getting that sleeping bag, which seemed even more desirable after the investment I had already made in terms of time and driving expense. At the conclusion of the tour, I was asked whether I was ready to sign on the dotted line for one of their $6000 camp spots. When I indicated that I would have to think that one over for awhile, they thanked me and said that they would keep in touch with me. When I asked them about the "free sleeping bag," they said, "Well, we usually give them only to *serious* guests." You and I both know what "serious" meant: putting your name on the dotted line for the $6000 camp spot.

Deadline Sales Pitches

"Until you spend your money, it's yours!" This is a handy-dandy maxim that you can use to make life a lot easier for yourself. One of its most valuable uses is for resisting deadline sales pitches from salespeople. I recently quoted this maxim to a car salesman who informed me that the "fabulous" price that he was offering me on the car of my interest would cease to be available once I walked off the dealer's premises. I replied, "That's O.K. Until I spend my money, it's mine!" Once he heard that, he was shattered, because he knew that I was in control of the bargaining.

Always keep in mind the fact that if you don't buy an item at the time of an "irresistible" offer, you maintain the purchasing power that you would have lost by buying it, and you retain the opportunity to look for an even better price. What's more, there is a pretty high probability that if you return to the salespeople later on and offer them the sales price, they will take it. If they were willing to sell the item earlier for a reduced amount, why wouldn't they, at a later time, be willing to sell it nine times out of ten for the same amount, if you were standing there making an offer and ready to walk out the door if they didn't take it?

I had some friends who were interested in purchasing a home that they had toured. The selling price was $49,000. (That was a few years back, when real estate was lower priced; in addition, the home was several years old.) The real estate salesman informed them that this was a "terrific buy," and that if they didn't purchase it immediately, it would be snapped up by one of the other potential buyers. They asked my opinion of their intended purchase. I noticed several things about the home that I thought would cause them to regret the purchase of it later on. They thought that they could live with those flaws. However, when I reminded them that if they didn't spend the $49,000 on this particular house, they would have it to spend on some other house which they might like even better, that clinched their decision not to buy.

It's quite easy for a person to be lured by a deadline sales pitch. Compulsive shoppers are easy prey for this approach, and even financially conservative people sometimes allow themselves to be trapped by it. I have normally rational friends who lose all sense of reason at the sight of a "SALE" sign. But, the next time you are confronted by an "irresistible" sales price, remember, "If you don't spend your money, it's still yours."

Purls of Wisdom

Importance Of Taking Biology

Whenever school districts or the State Board of Education activate committees to designate the required curriculum, a shower of sparks is sure to be generated. The specialists in every subject matter area ever invented compete to get more instructional time for their subjects, and, interestingly, they all usually seem to be able to present compelling arguments for their positions. This situation creates an ongoing, perennial headache for the curriculum policy makers, who have to make the final decisions about what is going to be required and what is not.

I am now going to add fuel to the flames of curricular debate by suggesting a graduation requirement that does not exist in most of the school districts with which I am familiar. *A class in Biology should be required of every high school student.*

The importance of a knowledge of Biology arises out of the fact that we are biological organisms, which not only perform all of the functions of all living things, but we also have a delicate interaction with all of the other living things and non-living things in our environment. To assume that the majority of us humans can rely on the biology specialists to protect our biological interests is like assuming that we can rely on our banker to see to it that our personal finances are properly organized. Besides having specialists to inform us of major concepts and discoveries, it is imperative that the individual have a knowledge of

12

basic concepts in order to take care of the personal details.

Most school districts have a heavy emphasis on Social Studies requirements for graduation, with the idea being that we are a socially oriented species, and in order to get along in the world, we have to have a grasp of basic social concepts. I don't argue with that point of view, but I do tend to add that an understanding of basic biological concepts is essential to the wise development and application of social policies.

I have known students who were fluent in a foreign language, and who knew minute details about the country where their foreign language originated, but who didn't have the slightest idea of how genetic characteristics (including defective ones) are passed from one generation to another. And I have known students who were very familiar with the legislative battle to ban chlorofluorocarbons in aerosols, but who didn't understand the importance of the fact that most animals give off carbon dioxide and most plants give off oxygen.

It is time that curriculum policy makers acknowledge the fact that a study of Biology is important for biological beings such as ourselves.

Preaching Abstinence

Largely in response to the AIDS epidemic, many public school systems have decided to initiate instructional programs intended to help students protect themselves from the AIDS virus. Many districts have included, in their instructional programs, lessons on the advisability of using condoms, and some have even included instruction on *how* to use condoms properly. Those school districts which do not emphasize exclusively abstinence are under much pressure to emphasize abstinence, if not advocate it exclusively, as the way to prevent not only AIDS, but also pregnancy. Personally, I don't believe that the preaching of abstinence will be effective with a very large percentage of teenagers. I taught for many years at both the junior high school level and the senior high school level. Besides that, like most people, I was a teenager once myself, and had abundant opportunities to observe the other teenagers around me. The observations which I made during those periods of my life led me to conclude that the sex drive in teenagers is much stronger than most adults believe it to be. I suspect that the majority of the parents who are advocating the limiting of sex education to the preaching of abstinence have either forgotten what it was like to be a hormone-driven teenager, or else when they were teenagers, they had sub-average sex drives themselves. I'm not claiming that *all* teenagers have overwhelming sex drives, but I do

14

contend that *most* teenagers do, and that the sex drive is too strong to be counteracted effectively by the preaching of abstinence.

When I was teaching teenagers, I could virtually see the hormones flowing from my charges. Just one afternoon of observing a typical high school student body will confirm this for the astute adult observer. To limit AIDS control and pregnancy avoidance to the preaching of abstinence alone is to ignore physiological reality of average teenagers. Of course, there is a certain segment of the teenager population that has a sub-average sex drive, and that segment would undoubtedly be more amenable to the preaching of abstinence than would those with typical sex hormone levels. It's just not safe to assume that the majority of teenagers who receive indoctrination about abstinence are going to abstain from sex. It's much safer to assume that many of them will engage in sex despite the indoctrination, and for that group we need additional instruction, such as the use of condoms.

The sex drive probably originated in human beings for the purpose of assuring procreation and continuation of the species. Assuming that the sex drive probably evolved over a period of millions of years, it's unrealistic to expect that that drive will be counteracted by a few periods in school where abstinence is preached.

15

The Value Of A Broad Education

When asked for the secret to success by a young person, a wise man once said, "Get all of the education that you can get!" Another way of saying the same thing is, "Learn everything that you can possibly learn." It doesn't necessarily have to be through formal education, although formal education is one of the most efficient ways to learn a lot.

All other things being equal, the person with the greater skill or knowledge will be more successful in life, and that skill and knowledge can be gained through careful attention to and observation of every phenomenon and piece of information to which one is exposed. Events during my 65 years of life have convinced me that I learned something valuable from every course I ever took, even from the lowest quality courses. And I have always felt that if I learned even one useful fact or skill from a course, that made the course worthwhile. In reality, we often don't find the fact or skill to be useful until years after we have learned it.

One phenomenon that seems to be almost universal among students is that each one prefers certain types of courses and tends to avoid certain other types. Many students get isolated in their majors, and thus lose the opportunity to gain useful knowledge and skills that may lie outside their major fields of study. My experience has shown that some of the most obscure facts learned in courses outside my field of personal interest can often be very useful in later life. That is why I strongly recommend that students take, in addition to the standard core of courses in their major field, a selection of survey courses in a wide variety of academic departments, even ones that they abhor.

My first seven years of college were spent in the field of Fisheries, with emphasis on biological science courses. My last year was spent in the field of Education. I am now able to conclude that I was fortunate that I had the opportunity and/or non-major requirement to take survey courses in several fields. They included, but were not limited to, Business Law, Geology, Music Appreciation, German, Astronomy, and Psychology. As an example of how these courses proved to be useful in later life, let me take the first, Business Law. At the time I was enrolled in the course, I could hardly wait for it to end, because it was a non-major requirement, and I was more oriented to the sciences than to the non-sciences. However, the knowledge that I gained from that course proved to be useful many times over in later life. One example of that is the time I saved myself $12,000 by having the basic business law skill needed to prove to my local water district that my parcel of land could support only two homes, not the five that they wanted to assess me for.

So, I say to all young people, "Learn all that you can learn, even if you think that it will never be useful."

17

Teaching Communication Skills

The schools cannot do an effective job of teaching good communication skills if those skills are not practiced in the students' homes. Instruction in punctuation and conjugation in the classroom will probably have little lasting influence if the students are widely exposed to communication at home in which almost every sentence is punctuated by "Y'know" or by references to conjugation of another sort. When you consider the fact that most students spend no more than an hour each day in instruction on proper usage of language, it is not surprising that the level of communication skills of the average high school graduate in the United States horrifies most employers.

The ability of people to communicate effectively affects not only their vocational success, but also their success as useful members of our society. Generally, those people who communicate clearly are much more well accepted by the community at large than those who don't. "So," you might ask, "how do we go about improving the communication skills of our citizenry?" Well, for one, perhaps communication skills should not be taught in isolation from the other subjects in school, but should be integrated with those subjects. That way, the exposure to communication training would be expanded from about one hour per day to five or six hours per day.

The solution to the problem of the influence of poor communication skills in the home is much more elusive. One answer might be to lengthen the school day, so that the students are under the direct influence of the school for a longer period each day. Another might be to have total-family communication training offered during after-school hours, so that the entire family could work together on communication skills. It would have to be voluntary, of course.

Employers have for a long time been aware of the advantages of good communication skills. Just look at the people who tend to rise to the top in various fields of endeavor. They are usually people with better than average communication skills. Workers who have below average communication skills tend to be stuck near the bottom of the career ladder in most fields of work.

One of the most important skills that parents can pass on to their offspring is that of good communication. It appears to me that families that have several generations of highly successful members often can attribute their success to the above average communication skills that they have passed on from one generation to the next. If you want to start now on the process of building a valuable family legacy, it might be wise to begin with assessing and improving your own communication skills.

What About Free Condoms In Schools?

Handing out free condoms in schools is too likely to convey the message that premarital sex is condoned, even encouraged! Not only that, most kids are like most adults: offer them anything free, and they'll grab it up. Then they'll try to figure out what to do with it. In the case of condoms, "what to do with it" is just a matter of "doin' what comes natcherly" for hormone-driven teenagers.

No, let's not distribute free condoms. Instead, let's put a condom machine in every public restroom in America. And of course we should make sure that the price of the condoms in those machines is low enough (say a quarter) that even kids below the poverty level can afford to protect themselves against the HIV scourge. Pricing poor kids out of the condom market would be virtual homicidal discrimination!

And I'm not talking about putting the machines in only boys' restrooms. Female condoms should be at the ready in the girls' restrooms, too. The female condom is one of the greatest boons to sex equity that has ever been invented. Now it isn't only the boys who can subtly display those telltale bulges in their wallets.

Yes, pay-for-play condoms in all public restrooms would help to avoid the permissiveness connotation of free condoms. Also, they would undoubtedly make teenagers more appreciative of the consequences of their actions. It is a commonly quoted notion that kids appreciate something more if they have to earn it. With that in mind, parents might want to require that their kids pay for *their own* condoms with *their own* money. However, this strategy will work only on kids who have learned the value of condom usage. Those parents whose offspring are unable to learn this beneficial bit of wisdom might want to slip the kids a quarter now and then.

Many opponents of easy condom availability point out that any kid who really wants a condom can get one at just about any drugstore. Well, most of the teenagers that *I* know would rather risk almost certain death from AIDS than to face the piercing stare of the drugstore clerk when they take their condoms to the checkout counter.

Promoting Democracy

Aiding non-democratic countries is not the most effective way to promote democracy. We should issue an ultimatum to all non-democracies that are currently receiving U.S. aid: Make significant progress toward democratic government within five years from this point, or our aid to your country will stop! The same ultimatum should be delivered to those so-called democratic countries in which there are flagrant abuses or denial of human rights.

The United States has gotten itself into extensive trouble by aiding non-democracies. The typical scenario is familiar:

1. We give foreign aid to a government that denies democratic participation and/or basic human rights to its citizens.
2. The citizenry rises up in revolt against the government policies and establishes a new populist government.
3. The new government denounces previous U.S. aid to its oppressive predecessor, and, on that basis, proceeds to promote anti-U.S. sentiment among its citizenry.

A sticking point for the proposed new policy is the fact that the U.S. is dependent upon several non-democratic countries for critical raw materials. That fact makes it appear unwise to implement such a policy. In actuality, we should begin right now to eliminate those dependencies. Then the policy will be more feasible.

An example of our dependency upon a non-democratic country is the case of Kuwait. Since the Iraq War, during which the U.S. expended tremendous amounts of human and financial resources in order to liberate Kuwait, numerous reports of human rights abuses have been flowing from that country. We would like to see those abuses stopped, but our thirst for Kuwaiti oil causes us to forego an aggressive approach in our dealings with the rulers of Kuwait. If we could achieve complete independence of foreign oil, we would not only be in a better position to demand reforms in Kuwait, but we could also be more effective in applying pressure for democratic reforms in other countries which currently supply us with oil that we need to keep our society functioning.

An essential first step in applying the recommended new democracy-promoting policy to all non-democratic countries is that of establishing U.S. independence in regard to all strategic raw materials that are currently supplied to us by non-democratic countries. We should begin now.

We're Threatening Our Survival By Damaging The Environment

For all practical purposes, the environment of human beings today is limited to the solid and aqueous surface of the earth, and the attendant atmosphere. One of the main reasons that humans have been so successful in comparison to other living species is that they have the greatest ability of all species to modify their environment to meet their own needs. Unfortunately, that success has resulted in the creation of a problem that is relatively new in comparison to the long existence of the human race. That is that our race has, in effect, overpopulated the earth, and in doing so, has damaged the environment severely, possibly irreparably and irreversibly. The damage of which I speak has resulted from the by-products of human activity. Some of the more noticeable and highly publicized forms of damage are the hole in the ozone, the greenhouse effect, air pollution, and water pollution. However, humans have caused innumerable other forms of damage to the environment, both dramatic and subtle.

In order to narrow the focus of this discussion, I would like to select one specific form of environmental damage for further discussion. That one is air pollution. Air pollution is most noticeable in some of the larger cities of the world, where, in some cases, people can't even go outdoors at times because of the dangers created by the polluted air. Although the harmful levels of air pollution are the result of too many by-products of too many people living in a limited area, one almost never reads or hears suggestions that the human population be reduced. Instead, attempts are made to solve the problem of air pollution through what I will call secondary measures. That is, instead of facing directly the basic problem of overpopulation, and doing something about the numbers of humans living in the polluted area, governments take secondary measures, such as requiring catalytic converters on all automobiles and banning woodburning stoves. A similar secondary approach can be identified in regard to other forms of environmental pollution and damage, also. That is, governments treat the secondary problems rather than the primary problem of excess human population.

For all we know, the excessive human population may have already damaged the environment irreversibly. For example, it may be that some of the by-products of human activity, specifically some of the particulate and gaseous pollutants in the atmosphere, have already changed the atmosphere in such a way that certain types of life (perhaps humans, themselves) will gradually die out entirely, because of their intolerance for those pollutants.

If the living organisms currently in existence on earth evolved in concert with an unpolluted atmosphere, then it is plausible to hypothesize that any significant change in that atmosphere could lower the survivability of those organisms. And what has changed the atmosphere most of all? It has been the by-products of human activity.

25

Productivity

The best way to achieve a truly healthy economy is to develop a cheap, unlimited source of energy. Most economists know that productivity is the key to a healthy economy. They realize that, generally, those countries which have the highest level of productivity among their citizens are the best off from the standpoint of both financial well-being and standard of living (which are not necessary synonymous). However, I have never yet heard of an economist who pointed out the relationship between the cost of energy and productivity. (Perhaps some have said it, and I'm just ignorant of that fact.) Most literate people know that energy from a variety of sources, such as hydroelectric dams and fossils fuels, to name two of the principal sources, can be harnessed for the purpose of running machinery. And, almost everyone knows that machines can be used to increase the productivity of people. Well, then, isn't it logical to assume that if we had unlimited cheap energy to run our machines, we could significantly increase human productivity? One could extrapolate from the foregoing points the idea that if we wanted to increase the standard of living of everyone, we should increase our efforts to identify a cheap, unlimited source of energy. Two of the most promising potential sources at the present time are solar power and fusion power. One very appealing factor in both of them is that they result in practically no harm to the environment. On

26

the other hand, our current two main sources of energy, hydroelectric power and fossil fuels, result in extensive damage to the environment. Hydroelectric dams cause deleterious warming of river waters, blockage of fish migration routes, and destruction of fish-spawning areas. The use of fossil fuels releases tremendous quantities of pollutants into the atmosphere and increases the levels of carbon dioxide.

Of course, the development of a cheap, unlimited source of energy would not be looked upon with enthusiasm by the owners of the world's fossil fuel reserves. That development would have an impact on the price of coal and oil comparable to what would happen to the price of gold if someone were to announce the invention of an inexpensive process for converting one of the more abundant and least expensive elements into gold.

The bottomline on this cheap-energy-standard-of-living relationship is that if we had an almost free and unlimited source of energy, everyone on earth could be assured of a relatively high standard of living- probably one at least equivalent to that which the middle-class American family now enjoys. And that is saying a lot, considering the fact that the middle-class American family is probably in the top one per cent as compared to the standard of living of everyone in the world.

Let's Teach Ethics In Our Public Schools

L ately, there has been a lot of discussion about the concept of "separation of church and state," particularly as it applies to the use of public funds for teaching religion in the schools of the United Sates. Thus far, the United States Supreme Court has made decisions which prohibit such use. The decisions have even gone so far as to prohibit *prayer* in public schools. Many religious organizations have been pressuring the court and congress to make changes in those decisions, so that public funds could be used in schools where religion is taught or where prayer is offered.

Realizing that the law will probably never be changed in that manner, I offer an alternative approach. It may be that many of the proponents of the teaching of religion in public schools are people who value the moral principles of religion just as much as the spiritualistic aspects. That type of person might settle for the teaching of "ethics" rather than religion. (The dictionary defines ethics as "the science of moral principles.") If it turned out that a majority of the U.S. population could accept the teaching of ethics in public schools, I think that such a concept would *not* be rejected by the Supreme Court. Of course, in making such a statement, I am distinguishing the difference between ethics and religion, even though there is a fine line of distinction.

That type of compromise might satisfy the vast majority of all of the various religious and non-religious groups in the country. It would give the schools an opportunity to teach valuable *moral* lessons, even though they couldn't teach spiritualistic lessons.

If ethics became an approved part of the public school curriculum, a starting point for organizing an instructional program might be to examine all of the world's religions, and to find out what the vast majority of them have in common. In making such a study of the world's religions, I found that almost all of them embody, among other things, the Golden Rule and respect for the rights of others. Of course, we would have to recognize the fact that some individual religious group might have an objection to one or more of the moral principles that are embraced by the vast majority. We should not allow that fact to scuttle the attempt to design an acceptable program of ethics instruction, since this concept, like most others in our democracy, would be determined by majority vote.

There is a chance that the inclusion of required instruction in ethics in the schools that use public funds could have a profound affect on our society. After all, I doubt that a very high percentage of the violent criminals in our country ever spent much time thinking about moral principles. If they had, I feel that the incidence of crime would be much lower than it is.

A Great Investment Opportunity

If you want a sure-fire long-term way to make money, start buying up abandoned garbage dumps. At the rate that our society is pillaging the planet and consuming critical raw materials, your investment might even end up having a short-term payoff.

Consider the fact that every time you throw away a "tin" can or a worn-out tire, you are throwing away not only large amounts of iron or rubber, respectively, but you are also discarding small amounts of eventually endangered trace elements.

And don't discount the potential value of even discarded plastic or Styrofoam containers. As soon as the earth is denuded (which may be sooner than you think) of its forests , and we cease to have the readily available source of long-chain carbon raw materials that they now provide, science will probably reveal a feasible way of utilizing those seemingly undegradeable objects as food for our materials-hungry manufacturing plants.

If you want to maximize your return, you should invest mainly in the *older* garbage dumps, the ones that are now discreetly covered by parks and golf courses. That is because they were filled at a time when conservation and recycling were practically unheard of; consequently, they should yield the richest hoard of useful elements.

And, of course, *American* garbage dumps should

be the main focus of your investment, since the throw-away society has reached its zenith in the United States. You would be foolhardy to invest in garbage dumps in a country like Bangladesh. The citizens there have never had the fun of throwing things away like we have. I guess it is only natural that one tends to hold on to even seemingly useless objects when one doesn't know where his next meal is coming from.

The only breakthrough that is needed (and one that is sure to come) in order to give garbage dumps inestimable value is the technology for a machine-driven, automatic process for reclaiming *unsorted* garbage. Several cities and counties already have found markets for certain items in *sorted* garbage, but the sorting is a minimally profitable, labor-intensive procedure.

So forget your mutual funds, your investment homes, your blue chip stocks. Cash them in now, and purchase instead some of the choice garbage dumps, before they have all been snapped up by investors who are quicker and wiser than yourself. If the world population continues to expand at its present rate, we ought to reach, in just a few short years, a zero-supply-level of many of the critical raw materials, which lie waiting to be reclaimed from the world's garbage dumps.

Controlling The Goose Population

We have a problem with excess geese around lakes, parks, and beaches. They have appeared in increasing numbers in recent years, mainly as a result of extensive expansion of "No Hunting" areas. The Canada goose is a majestic bird, one that is pleasing to watch as it soars through the air and glides through the water. However, its droppings foul the spots where it resides, and that detracts from people's enjoyment of those places.

In response to numerous citizen complaints about the geese fouling recreational areas in the western portion of the state of Washington, the Department of Wildlife has begun a program of trapping the geese and shipping them off to eastern Washington and Idaho. Although that plan may seem good to some, many animal protectionists vociferously oppose meddling with the life style of any animal, including the goose. Personally, I doubt that the goose protectionists have ever experienced great gobs of goose goo all over their new Nike's. They prefer to gamble with our public health by letting the geese gambol all over our recreational areas.

Aside from the protectionists' opposition to the trapping-shipping idea, it has a serious flaw that will probably cause it to fail, anyway. Consider the fact that the Canada goose normally ranges as far north as Alaska in the summer, and as far south as Mexico in the winter. Now, if the geese can find their way from

Alaska to Mexico and back, what makes the wildlife biologists think that they can't find their way back to western Washington from eastern Washington and Idaho?

No, shipping the geese over the pass is not the answer. There is at hand, however, a flicker of hope for a practical solution to the goose population problem. It stems from the successful efforts to control the pigeon populations in many of our large cities by feeding the pigeons grain laced with pigeon-birth-control hormone. If a birth control hormone potion can be developed for pigeons, it doesn't seem too unrealistic to expect the development of a comparable diet supplement for the Canada goose. Then, when our children visit the beaches, instead of being confronted by signs that say, "Please don't feed the fouling fowl!," they could happily toss their hormone-laced goose food (supplied by the Wildlife Department, of course) to the unsuspecting geese, which would gleefully gobble it up.

Of course, not everyone would be satisfied with this arrangement. Some ultra-protectionists would be unhappy about it, because they don't want us humans interfering with the "inalienable right" of all living things to reproduce unlimited numbers of offspring. Personally, I don't think that the geese know *what* their rights are!

The Proportion Of Defective Genes Is Increasing

Today, many humans are able to survive and reproduce successfully despite having genetic abnormalities that would have prevented their survival in periods of human existence prior to about the last 100 years. One single, simple example is diabetes. I feel safe in mentioning it, since most of the members of the last two generations of my ancestors had diabetes. As far as we know, diabetes is caused by a genetic abnormality which may have resulted from a gene mutation far back in the development of the human race. Before insulin and its substitutes were discovered relatively recently in human history, the majority of people with diabetes didn't survive to the stage at which they reproduced successfully. Therefore, the gene that causes diabetes was "selected against;" that is to say, the individuals who possessed the diabetes gene to the extent that they manifested diabetes had a slim chance of surviving to the reproductive stage.

The ensuing discovery of insulin treatment greatly increased the survivability of diabetics. It has permitted diabetics to lead relatively normal lives, which includes reproducing successfully. And, the diabetic's offspring may very well inherit the abnormal diabetes gene which was in the genetic makeup of the parent. The net result is that, since the discovery of insulin, the proportion of diabetes genes in the human population has undoubtedly been increasing.

There are many other disabilities, illnesses, and diseases that are caused by so-called "defective" genes. It is also true that, as with diabetes, many of those conditions are now being ameliorated successfully through medical treatment. And, as with diabetes, it is plausible to contend that the medical treatment is increasing the probability that the sufferers of those conditions will reproduce successfully. Thus, their causative genes are also likely to increase in proportion in the human gene pool.

If you believe my hypothesis that the proportion of defective genes in the human gene pool is increasing, you might tend to ask what can be done to reverse that trend. One answer would be to deny medical treatment to those who exhibit the manifestations of the defective genes. Their type would soon die out of the population. Another answer would be to require reproductive sterilization of all people who possess the defective genes. Both of those answers suggest a Hitler-like approach to the problem. I have never met a single human being who accepted those ideas.

Economic Growth

E conomic growth isn't all good! Of course, you would never know that by examining the business pages of the local newspaper. In practically every column of that section, growth is touted as the economic salvation for our society. Just one more point of rise in the GDP, so the myth goes, will solve all of our problems. Well, the GDP has been rising since time immemorial, and the vast majority of our population still needs not only "just a few more dollars," but a lot more common sense and basic values.

Actually, instead of being called the Gross Domestic Product, the GDP should stand for Gross Domestic Plundering. In large part, it is a measure of the degree to which we are pillaging our environment. The rate at which we can produce manufactured goods is considered to be an accurate measure of our societal success, when in reality it measures our success in stripping the earth of many of its non-renewable critical raw resources. Every automobile or airplane that rolls off the assembly line brings the human population closer to the day when the essential materials for those creations are too scarce to support their manufacture.

As long as a nation has abundant sources of raw materials and expansive markets for their goods, a high GDP probably does indicate national wealth. But, what happens if the sources of raw materials dry up or the markets disappear. In the first place, it would be pretty difficult to attain a high GDP, and secondly, the high GDP wouldn't do any good, because few of the products could be sold. Of course, many economists adhere to the idea that if you can't find external markets, you can encourage a high rate of reproduction in your own country, so as to create your own markets internally. However, a high birth rate creates a whole host of problems which are counterproductive to a high GDP. They include, but are not limited to overloads on the educational system, high crime rates, expanded intrusion of government into individual privacy, and increased rates of taxation, among many.

Perhaps we should replace the hallowed goal of high Gross Domestic *Product* with high Gross Domestic *Productivity.* Although the difference may be imperceptible to some, it is significant. The former is measured in quantitative terms of products that are turned out and sold, and it is dependent on an expanding population. The latter can be only roughly estimated in terms of relatively intangible things that we do, not only for ourselves, but for others as well, and it could reach its ultimate peak within the existing population level. The indicator of Gross Domestic Productivity would include an assessment of all of the humane and humanitarian things that every individual does for the good of society as a whole.

No, economic growth is not the societal panacea that many consider it to be. Let's take it down off its pecuniary pedestal and replace it with a goal of growth in morality and mankind's humaneness to mankind.

Our Environment Is Not Infinite

During the first half of the twentieth century, the primary concern of population experts was the question of how to feed the burgeoning population of the earth. Extensive efforts were undertaken to increase the productivity of the world's farms and farmers, and to increase the food supply in other ways, also. Little thought was given to cutting down on the birth rate, and to thus keep the population level from straining the food supply. During those years, people tended to look upon the earth as an infinite environment: one that could support unlimited population growth. In recent years, however, it has become apparent that the environment is not infinite.

One important way to measure the progress of the human race is in terms of their standard of living. Up until recent years, the standard of living of any group of people was closely related to both their control of the environment and to their utilization of various aspects of the environment, including raw materials. As long as the environment was "effectively" infinite, that approach was reasonable, but now we have to examine other alternatives for preserving and enhancing our standard of living. No longer can we enhance it by plundering the environment, because there are so many of us on earth now, that every time one group over-utilizes the environment, that has one or more adverse effects on some other group. One fairly familiar example is the interdependence between our forestry and fisheries industries. For years we logged off the trees as though there were no end to the supply. As a result, water run-off from former timberlands increased extensively, causing two primary effects. One was the rise in the temperature of streams. The other was an increase in siltation of the stream beds due to soil erosion on the denuded lands. The higher temperatures have resulted in extensive loss of fish life in the streams, and the siltation has caused a loss of much of the prime fish spawning areas. The logging of the timber created numerous jobs for the people of the area, but the lowered fish population has eliminated numerous other jobs in the fisheries industry. That is only one of many examples that I can think of which illustrate the interdependence between various segments of our environment, and what happens when the human population over-utilizes one segment of it. If we had an infinite environment, the human population could spread out widely throughout it, and thus humans might not have any significant negative effects on each other. But, the environment is not infinite; therefore the more that the population increases, the greater the effects that humans have on other humans.

I think that it's safe to say that a finite environment cannot support an unlimited human population, and it's time that world leaders acknowledged that fact.

Fighting Litter

If we want to completely rid the environment of litter, we're going to have to give the human population greater motivation not to throw away packaging materials. That may mean making every scrap and particle of our wrappings or containers so valuable that either people would not want to throw them away, or even if they did, someone else would be interested in picking up the stuff. As we all know, there are some packaging materials which currently have significant salvage value because they are composed of substances that can be easily and profitably recycled. One example is the aluminum beverage can. Another is the glass container, which most recycling centers have found to produce a profit. However, neither one of the aforementioned types of packaging materials is recycled and salvaged to the degree that it ought to be if we want to eliminate it totally from the litter that is deposited along our highways and elsewhere. On top of that, there is the fact that most *other* types of packaging materials are practically non-recyclable, and they are discarded with even higher rates of frequency. Some of the more prevalent items in this category are the plastic and paper ones.

So, the question arises as to what we have to do to make all packaging materials, including the plastic and paper ones, worth recycling or salvaging. Well, I think I have the answer that will make even the tiniest packaging, like a gum wrapper, sufficiently valuable to cause someone to want to pick it up. Let's add a relatively valuable substance to all packaging materials. It could be incorporated into the fabric of woven items, or it could be scattered as granules in cast or molded items. The first such substance to come to mind is gold, although there may be a sufficiently valuable, yet more easily reclaimable material that would serve the intended purpose. Whatever we use, it should be separable by automated mass-separation processes.

We also need to decide upon the minimum value to be required of even the smallest packaging unit. A nickel might be acceptable; there are still people in the world who will make the effort to stoop over and pick up something if it is worth a nickel. A penny is a different story.

Naturally, the packaging manufacturers would strongly resist this whole idea. It could force them to raise drastically the prices of their products. Many business owners would probably react in a similar fashion. However, in the truly democratic way, they could just pass the cost on to the consumer.

A side-benefit to this approach would be the entire new industry and source of income that would be generated in the form of people combing the countryside for gold-laden packaging materials. The salvaging and recycling of litter might even become a noble occupation.

41

The Dangers Of Motorcycles

M otorcycles are not dangerous! It's the drivers that are dangerous! The relatively high rate of mortality among motorcycle operators as compared with operators of automobiles is not because the motorcycle is inherently a more dangerous vehicle than the automobile. More than likely it is because many a normal, sane automobile driver is suddenly transformed into a motorized maniac when he gets behind the handlebars of a motorcycle. The Casper Milquetoast in your average male is replaced by a driving daredevil the moment he slips into the saddle of a Harley or Honda.

You may notice that I tend to use the male gender when I discuss this topic. That is because the macho machine under discussion appears to have a greater tendency to arouse the automotive animal in men, moreso than in women. That is not to say that I haven't observed a female fool on two wheels a time or two.

Some of the traffic laws which are routinely obeyed by the average automobile driver are like a gauntlet thrown at the feet of the same people when the latter get on a two-wheeler. A few of their favorite antics are passing on curves and hills, passing on the shoulder of the roadway, suddenly cutting in between two tightly-spaced cars, and accelerating to pass in the face of swift, oncoming traffic. The thrill of such risk-taking seems to be overwhelming to a large percentage of motorcycle drivers, and blinds them to the reality of increased likelihood of a premature demise.

A fairly accurate predictor of the amount of risk that a motorcycle driver is inclined to take is the level of decibels of the sound that is given off by the respective motorcycle's engine. The next time you observe a motorcycle operator taking an extreme risk, notice the amount of sound which his motorcycle emits. You can almost bet that it will be in the high decibel range. If the whine of the motorcycle is barely audible, you can be pretty sure that the driver is among the more conservative ones.

So, lady, if your spouse drives a motorcycle, and if its exhaust gives off a blast that shakes the neighbors out of their easy chairs, you would be well advised to rush out and increase the face value of his life insurance policy. The chances are pretty good that he is a roadway renegade who will soon be a freeway fatality.

What Is Music?

The definition of music has been expanded in recent years to include some fairly far-fetched forms of entertainment. The imagination has to be stretched beyond reasonable bounds in order to accept as music some of the types of performances that some of the so-called "musicians" offer us. Therefore, I would like to offer what a scientist might call "an operational definition" of music, but in the negative form: "It isn't music if it can't be whistled or hummed." Back in my day, music was what was played on the "Hit Parade" every Saturday night. It was what was sung around the campfire on a summer outing. It was what you went to the symphony to listen to. The tunes that we heard on those occasions were real music! A mother could hum those tunes to her children at bedtime. A guy in love could whistle those tunes that reminded him of his sweetheart. Some of today's more inane utterances like heavy metal and rap just don't fit my operational definition of music. I defy any mom to hum heavy metal, and I challenge any guy to whistle rap.

I know one public school music teacher who is acutely frustrated in his attempts to teach his students musical skills and music appreciation. The current crop of kids finds rap far more appealing than Beethoven and Bach, or even Berlin and Bacharach. I guess his definition of music must be similar to mine. Of course he and I grew up during a time when you could understand the words to a song without switching it to slow-play. Kids nowadays prefer audio expressionism that we adults are unable to decipher without a teenage interpreter.

There is one author who has postulated the possibility that the evolution of our music determines the course of societal development. Well, if that's the case, where are the non-music of heavy metal and rap leading us? If the author's postulate is correct, perhaps we should outlaw heavy metal and rap, and require school instruction in jazz, swing, and easy listening music, which seem to have preceded less hectic times. That might be one way to turn our society around from the spiraling decline it has experienced during the last few years.

Creating Non-biodegradeable Substances

Sprinkled liberally throughout the advertising in the news media these days are articles extolling the virtues of newly invented products that will last for long periods of time. In this regard, we hear phrases like "long-lasting," "corrosion-resistant," and "durable." Another, less-used phrase that describes many of these types of products is "non-biodegradeable." The latter phrase is not heard nearly as much in advertising as is the phrase *"biodegradeable."* Just about everyone knows that *"biodegradeable "* in advertising connotes something good about a product.

Unfortunately, the human species has the greatest capacity of all living species for creating non-biodegradeable substances. Many scientists have, in fact, labored extensively for the purpose of creating non-biodegradeable materials. In some cases it was for the purpose of gaining the specific advantage of long-lived products; in others, it was for the purpose of creating products that were less expensive than previously utilized alternatives. Just two examples of materials that have achieved both of these objectives are PVC pipe and plastic packaging materials. Unfortunately (or fortunately, depending upon your point of view) the latter are so inexpensive that their utilization has multiplied geometrically.

"Well," you might say, "what is so important about the fact that humans are creating a lot of non-biodegradeable substances?" The answer is that the earth is a finite ecosystem, believe it or not, and in a finite ecosystem, chemical molecules of the elements that are needed by the living things in that ecosystem are in a continuing cycle of being built up into useful compounds and then being broken down again into the basic molecular form, only to be re-used by other living things. Most living organisms don't have the capability of taking chemical molecules out of this cycle by converting them into non-biodegradeable substances. However, human beings have the very unique manufacturing capability that I mentioned earlier, and the human population has now gotten to the point where it is locking huge amounts of useful chemical molecules into virtually unavailable compounds practically forever. A very disadvantageous side-effect of that process is that it adds to the ever-increasing expansion of the world's garbage dumps, that contain huge proportions of discarded materials that are non-biodegradeable, and which will never disappear entirely.

If you are a person that is concerned not only about the welfare of humanity today, but also about the quality of life of future generations, all of the foregoing discussion should seem relevant to you.

The Perils Of Population Growth

The human population is headed for self-destruction! That is, unless it reverses the current trend in the birth rate. The latter notion is, of course, considered to be heresy among many groups in our human society. Most people consider the right to unchecked reproduction to be an inalienable one that can be practiced without question, and many of them implement it in the face of woefully inadequate financial, psychological, and physical resources.

There are, of course, some religious denominations that aggressively promote rapid reproduction. But, in addition, many other people, without that influence, actively strive to produce as many offspring as they can. Then, on top of that, there is the whole group of humans that doesn't actually know what causes babies to be conceived, and that group goes on producing one offspring after another, even though they may not be able to properly raise them for one reason or another.

Not only is a major proportion of the human population either consciously or unconsciously contributing to the overpopulation of the earth, but there are those from the "old school" of economics who promote the idea of a high birth rate, contending that it is the only way to have a healthy economy. They are the ones who daily eye the GDP and the Index of Leading Economic Indicators. They include a lot of business people, who would find their own personal economy to be negatively affected by a decrease in the population, even though the overall human societal economy might in actuality be better off.

Most of the people discussed in the foregoing paragraphs are seemingly unaware of the relationship between birth rate and a whole host of phenomena which they consider to be problems. Notable examples are the following: the crime rate; the pollution of the atmosphere; the over-expansion of garbage dumps; homelessness; governmental usurpation of individual rights; the spread of contagious diseases; increased tax rates; food shortages; and water shortages. In actuality, every one of those "problems" is actually a symptom that can be traced to the basic problem of overpopulation. And everyone of them has the potential for either wiping out life on earth or at least significantly reducing the quality of human life. However, it appears that the average human being is incapable of comprehending that relationship. So, as a result, instead of solving the basic *problem* of overpopulation, we treat the numerous *symptoms* through temporary "drip-bucket" measures. (You know, the drip-bucket that is placed under the roof leak in order to "solve" the leak!)

Is It Racial Or Cultural Discrimination?

Much of what is called "racial" discrimination may actually be "cultural" discrimination. First, let's examine the meaning of the word "discrimination." According to the dictionary, the word "discrimination" means "the act or quality of distinguishing." One of the rights that we value in our American society is the right to choose our friends and associates. And, that process is based on differences which we distinguish between those with whom we choose to associate, as opposed to those with whom we choose not to associate. I think it is safe to say that just about everyone distinguishes, or "discriminates" in that way. And most would argue that that right should be maintained. The only time that discrimination becomes insidious is when it is based on human traits that are beyond the ability of the individual to change, such as racial characteristics.

Getting back to the original topic, racial discrimination is usually interpreted to be that type of discrimination that is based upon hereditary skin color or other kinds of racial characteristics. It is interesting to note that the majority of people in some races are not only different in hereditary characteristics from the people of other races, but they also have different *cultural* characteristics. By cultural characteristics, I mean behaviors that are a matter of tradition, and

more importantly, choice. I feel that cultural d
ences can cause different races to be mutuall, ..
pelled just as much or more than hereditary racial
characteristics in many cases.

I, personally, have seriously attempted to overcome the types of prejudices which my family and
friends exhibited as I was growing up. And I think
that I have succeeded, for the most part, in overcoming my own feelings of racial discrimination. However, I have found it very difficult to overcome my
feelings of *cultural discrimination.* I find it very easy
to be completely accepting of a person from another
race if that person behaves in a dignified, intelligent,
and friendly manner. But, if I am exposed to a person
from another culture, and that person behaves in an
undignified or unintelligent or unfriendly manner, I
tend to be repulsed by that person's behavior. If that
person's behavior is characteristic of that person's
culture, I find it difficult to be accepting of *any* members of that person's culture. And, I feel confident that
a lot of other people feel the same way that I do

To sum it all up, let me say that there are some
specific cultures whose members I don't care to associate with, and I'm fairly certain that those people
aren't really interested in associating with me, either.
So, it can probably be said that we are exhibiting
cultural discrimination. But, if we happen to be of
different races, does that mean that we are also prac-
ticing *racial* discrimination? I don't think so!

Who's Going To Pay For What?

If you thought NIMBYs were a bane to society, wait till you hear about SECPAYs. As you probably already know, NIMBYs (Not In My Back Yard) are those people who vociferously oppose any project that is a threat, either real or imaginary, to their current way of life. (And in many cases, the threat is of the "imaginary" type.) The NIMBY's attention is most notably focused upon garbage dumps and jails, which are usually large, governmental projects; but, in actuality, no project is too small to escape scrutiny by the NIMBYs. The hallmark of NIMBYs is, of course, that they don't usually mind questionable projects being carried out; they just don't want them located in their own localities.

In more recent times, SECPAYs have begun appearing upon the scene in increasing numbers. SECPAYs (Someone Else Can Pay) are the next of kin of NIMBYs. The hallmark of SECPAYs is that they feel totally justified in expecting someone else to pay for their pet projects. The most highly publicized SECPAY projects of late have been some of the brand new, exceedingly expensive, and sometimes experimental medical procedures. I'm talking here about procedures to correct ailments that we accepted living with (or dying with) just a few short years ago. The most common financial targets of SECPAYs have tended to be governments at all levels and insurance companies. As we all know, those entities have unlimited financial resources. In order to raise the funds for the SECPAY's favorite projects, all a government has to do is raise taxes on the rich. Insurance companies, on the other hand, get their funds for SECPAY projects by either raising their rates or by increasing the speed of their approach toward bankruptcy, either one of which threatens their very existence in the long run. By the SECPAY way of thinking, increased insurance rates are a convenient way to spread the costs of their project over the total population, so that hardly anyone notices the cost, theoretically. In actuality, a lot of people notice the cost, which is why *everyone* is complaining about skyrocketing rates.

SECPAYs often take undue advantage of the tendency of the press to publicize their types of projects. We view them in TV coverage of their emotional pleas to our basic sense of humaneness, and our reactions translate into "public pressure" for funds to be allocated. All the while, the standard of living of the public-at-large is eroded by the drain on financial resources toward which we all contribute in one way or another.

In order to deal with the rapidly expanding SECPAY phenomenon, I propose that we establish a mandatory Federal SECPAY Insurance Program (FedSECPIP), so that the costs of the SECPAY mentality are borne by all citizens, including SECPAYs.

Let's Get Realistic About Sexual Harassment

L et's get realistic! Women who dress in certain ways are inviting "sexual harassment." I contend that most girls don't have the foggiest notion about how the sight of certain elements of "stylish" women's attire is processed in the mental machinery of most men. One of the major cases in point is that of high-heeled shoes. Most women don't realize that the sight of a girl in high heels triggers an unbelievable surge of hormones in the male system. I suspect that the first woman in the world who ever wore high heels didn't take long to discover this phenomenon (although she may not have been aware of the physiological mechanism behind it), and from that point on, high heels were destined to be a part of the "stylish" woman's attire.

I expect a lot of people to challenge this view that I hold about high heels, but it was developed after long years of people watching. During my high school years, I was on several athletic teams, and got abundant opportunity to observe male locker-room behavior. During my college years, I resided in a very large organized housing group for men only, and witnessed the behavior patterns of the typical male college student. Later, when I was in the U.S. Army, I lived in a large barracks-type group with scores of men. You could take a dozen men from any of the aforementioned groups, and see the significant difference in their reaction to a woman walking by in high heels and that same woman walking by in flat-heeled walking shoes.

Some other male-hormone-triggers include women's clothing that emphasizes the breasts, short skirts that expose bare legs and thighs, and well-applied makeup. In regard to the latter, the story has it that Cleopatra knew the effect of red lips and rosy cheeks on men, and that her ability to use makeup effectively contributed in a big way to her success in luring Mark Anthony.

People who criticize men for their reactions to these hormone triggers ignore the fact that those reactions are built into the genetic makeup of the average human male. They probably developed over a period of thousands of human generations as part of the processes that helped to assure the procreation of the human species. Anyone who suggests that men completely cease their attentiveness to "suggestively-dressed" women is expecting the very unlikely process of the results of a million-plus years of male human evolution being reversed in just one generation.

Well, girls, the bottomline is if you don't want to be the recipients of sexually-oriented comments, put on those amorphous-looking blouses, baggy pants and flat-heeled walking shoes, and avoid all makeup. Under those conditions, I can almost guarantee that the typical human male will pay you little heed.

Building The Self-image

If your self-image is based on a fancy car, you're
in trouble! Actually, you could pick any other
status symbol, and the statement would be just as
true. Psychologists tell us that all people like to receive attention, although some crave it more than
others. Your typical self-image self-builder assumes
that a nice status symbol is an easy way to get attention. Conventional theory has it that if you can get a
little more attention, your self-image will rise a few
percentage points. Well, I don't go along with the
conventional wisdom on this point. After raising three
of my own children through infancy, teenhood, college, and up to marriage, and after having worked
with students from kindergarten through college age
for 32 years, I have concluded that status symbols are
actually an *ineffective* way to truly raise one's self-
image, at least on any kind of a permanent basis. It
appears to me that status symbols are like a drug for
the average human having a low self-image. A rather
low dosage of status symbol raises the self-image
noticeably at first, but after its effect begins to wear
off, it takes a stronger dose to renew the self-image.
The true status-symbol addict looks for an ever-increasing dosage to revive the ever-waning self-image.

One place where the craving for status symbols is
rampant is among the teenage population. It also
happens, perhaps not coincidentally, that that is the
phase during which most humans experience their

greatest period of self-doubt. One of the quickest ways to riches is to develop a status symbol item that becomes a teen fad, and which *every* teen "just has to have," and "only a nerd would be without one." That self-effacing population of juveniles proceeds to produce a fortune for the inventor of the fad item.

One of the things that I noticed during my many long years of parenting and educating, is that status symbols which are *given* to those with low self-images often have the reverse of the hypothesized stimulant effect on the self-image. The drug effect of the status symbol gift wears off very quickly, and simply leaves the person with a lower self-image than what was possessed previously. A lot of parents who are aware of their children's low self-image try to cure the problem by *giving* them status symbols. But what really happens is that the kids know subconsciously that the status symbol is one that was not earned, and so they go on a guilt trip over that realization. No, if you are going to permit your children to try to bolster their self-images with status symbols, at least require that they earn them themselves. Of course, it would be much better in the long run to try to wean them away from status symbols altogether, and to teach them that self-image is not something that one consciously builds, but is, instead, the natural result of a person's becoming a mature, worthwhile individual.

The Effects Of Overpopulation

The earth is just one giant terrarium! You might remember terrariums as those sealed glass chambers that Biology teachers use to demonstrate what happens if the plants and animals get out of balance in a finite ecosystem. If you put in too many animals, some of the animals die; if you put in too many plants, some of the plants die. The relationship between the animals and the plants is complex, but most Biology teachers simply explain it as a function of the oxygen-carbon dioxide cycle: plants use carbon dioxide and give off oxygen; animals use oxygen and give off carbon dioxide. Therefore, they mutually benefit each other. Too many animals deplete the oxygen supply; too many plants deplete the carbon dioxide supply.

After I observed what happened in the terrarium with too many animals in my high school Biology class in 1945, I asked the teacher whether there could ever be too many animals on the earth. His reply was what one might have expected in those pre-environmentalist years: "Never! The earth's environment is just too big for that to happen." Well, personally I think that he underestimated the ability of the human race not only to multiply, but also to denude the earth systematically of most of its vegetation.

The technology exists for controlling the human population in a humane manner. Sadly, the majority of the earth's human inhabitants are oblivious to the cause-and-effect relationship between overpopulation and a host of social, economic, and biological problems. And I think that they prefer to remain oblivious. It is much more relaxing to speculate about which team will win the Superbowl than to ponder the fate of an overpopulated world. Where our next paycheck is coming from is of greater immediacy than where our planet is going. Combine that kind of complacency with the fact that most humans feel that they have an inalienable right to reproduce to whatever extent they desire, and you have the scenario for a disaster that is beyond the comprehension of most people.

If we continue at the current pace of reproduction and forest destruction, we may be players in the most gigantic terrarium demonstration of all, and it will be the one with too many oxygen-consumers.

Knowing Where Our Belongings Are

There's not much advantage in owning some thing if you don't know where it is! If you don't know where one of your belongings is, how are you going to make use of it without wasting a lot of time looking for it. If there's anything that is the bane of human productivity, it seems to me to be the act of searching over and over for an item that you "know is here somewhere," but seems to be found "nowhere." I am the butt of frequent jokes about my "over-organization," which translates into the fact that I know where everything is that I own. Being a complete "nerd," I actually believe the old saying, "Everything in its place, and a place for everything." I didn't have to live to a very advanced age before I learned that if you knew where something was, it was a lot easier to find. Apparently, that concept is unfathomable by many of my friends, however. Most of them own more tools and assorted handy gadgets than I do, but guess who is borrowing from whom most of the time. For most people, it's a lot easier to borrow from their neighbor than to comb their own domicile for elusive equipment.

It appears to me that one of the principal repositories of belongings that can't be found is the family garage. Have you ever wondered why so many people park their cars *outside* their garages? Well, a tour of the neighborhood on a sunny Saturday afternoon when most families have their garage doors open during yard-maintenance time will reveal the answer to that mystery: Piles of confused conglomerations of all descriptions that have been assigned to oblivion in the garage "storage" area.

I must say at this point that I haven't yet succumbed to the ultimate temptation of painting black silhouettes behind the place where each tool and gadget is supposed to hang on a pegboard. I have a couple of super-organized friends that have done that. However, it turns out that they're not so super-organized that they remember to return each item to its rightful spot on the pegboard after using it. Well, at least they have the satisfaction of knowing what's missing, even if they can't find it.

I have one friend who is easily persuaded by advertising to buy every handy-dandy gadget in the world that might make his life a little easier. The trouble is, after he buys those items, he stores them in "unforgettable" locations which he then proceeds to forget. He would have a hard time convincing me that there's any advantage to him in owning all of those gadgets which he can't find.

The Best Bargains

Many advertisers would have you believe that the cheapest price results in the best bargain. That myth is promoted in sales of everything from aspirin to zippers. However, the astute shopper knows that there are many variables besides the price of a product that determine whether it is a bargain. Probably the most widely applicable variable is quantity: how much or how many you get for the monetary unit. In many grocery stores, a unit-pricing system has been adopted that facilitates price comparisons by shoppers. In the case of products or stores where unit pricing is not provided, the small hand-held calculator has greatly enhanced the customer's ability to make price comparisons. A few quick calculations can tell you whether one brand or the other gives you the best value for the money.

Another factor that determines the relative value of a product is the nature of the warranty. Warranties are routinely offered on the types of products which are customarily guaranteed against defects, breakdowns, or other problems. They are used primarily with products that tend to wear out under normal use. Generally, $\underline{I}$ assume that the length of the warranty that is offered by the manufacturer or the sales outlet indicates the relative degree of confidence that they have in the durability of the warranted product. For example, a washing machine that has a two-year warranty on parts and labor will probably go much longer without a breakdown than one that has only a one-year warranty, all other things being equal. However, the consumer is well-advised to read the fine print in all warranties, especially as they apply to very expensive items like major appliances and automobiles. "Slick" "fly-by-night" manufacturers or sales outlets know how to make warranties sound like they provide more protection than they actually do provide.

A third indicator of the value of a purchase is the amount of service that is offered with it. This is especially applicable to major products that require periodic service in order to prevent mechanical failure. For example, some automobile dealers offer various levels of free service of the types that are recommended by the manufacturers of the cars, and that free service cannot only save the buyer money, but also can help the purchaser to maintain a regular maintenance schedule which, in itself, can go a long way in preventing breakdowns. As with warranties, however, the purchaser is advised to read the fine print of service agreements, because they too can be worded so as to make the buyer think that they are getting more than they actually are getting.

The next time you're shopping for a specific item, try not to let yourself be distracted by only the purchase price and all of the clever machinations that sales people have learned to apply to it in order to lure unsuspecting consumers. And always remember that the cheapest price may not be the best bargain.

The Benefits Of Exercise

There is strong evidence that all human body organs need exercise in order to continue to function properly. I will take that one step further, and postulate that all human body organs need *peak* exercise in order to maintain the capability of *peak* performance.

As a volunteer entertainer who performs at numerous nursing homes and retirement homes, I have had an opportunity to observe large numbers of elderly citizens who have limited physical and/or mental capabilities. It appears that many of those limitations have been the result of medical conditions such as strokes, heart attacks, and Alzheimer's disease. But, there are indications that many of those people are limited simply because they failed to give their body organs adequate exercise. There is abundant evidence indicating that exercise can help elderly citizens to maintain their physical and mental abilities far above that which they would have without it. One such source is the AARP magazine *Modern Maturity*, which frequently presents scientifically based articles on the benefits of physical and mental exercise.

In conversations with fitness-center personnel, I have been told about remarkable physical comebacks by elderly people who started a fitness program long after their muscles had become greatly deteriorated by a lack of exercise. Those reports have indicated that we not only can prevent the reduction in our muscular strength by getting sufficiently frequent and strenuous exercise, but we can regain it by undertaking such exercise on a gradually increased basis even after it has been lost for the most part. One of the realities with which we are all faced is that after we have lost some of our abilities because of disuse of various body organs, it becomes even more difficult to undertake the necessary exercise. Therefore, it would probably behoove all of us to make sure that we maintain an adequate exercise program throughout life, so that our abilities to accomplish *further* exercise don't diminish.

To take the exercise/performance concept to far-reaching limits, I should mention the report that was published about some doctors who have found that prostate problems are more prevalent among elderly men who are *not* sexually active than it is among those who *are* sexually active. Could it be that the prostate gland is subject to the same general rule as many other body organs, and that it needs exercise in order to maintain its function? And if an organ which is under only involuntary control such as the prostate is, why not most other organs, too?

If the hypothesis that is implied here is accurate, one should consider giving *all* organs of the human body adequate exercise. Those include, but are not limited to the muscles, nervous-system organs, circulatory-system organs, and sex organs.

Birth Rate And Societal Problems

Many of the societal problems in today's world are the results of too high a human birth rate. The mechanism by which an excessive birth rate leads to societal problems is that the ratio of immature, poorly educated children to the more mature, better educated adults becomes much too high to permit adequate training and supervision of the former by the latter. The importance of this proportion is seen at various levels of our society, including but not limited to the individual family, the school classroom, and community teenage social organizations.

In the case of the family unit, having too many children can excessively strain the financial, emotional, and physical abilities of the parents to raise the children properly. In the school classroom, too high a ratio of students to teachers can result in a decrease in the quality of education. In the case of community social organizations, too high a ratio of non-adults to adults can result in extensive disregard for moral and legal principles.

The end result in the case of the family setting, is that the children often don't receive adequate guidance and training. In the school setting, the students often create discipline problems and demonstrate a low level of learning. And in the case of the community social organizations, gang-like behavior often surfaces.

In regard to the aforementioned problems, one

can point out exceptions to the general results which have been described, but we should not allow the existence of a few exceptions to deter us from making serious attempts to reduce the birth rate. I doubt that the problems of inadequate family upbringing, sub-average school education, and teenage delinquency will ever be overcome unless the ratio of children to adults in all units of our society is reduced to a point at which adult supervision of children is adequate.

Most of us tend to think of overpopulation as causing problems of environmental pollution, but there are other problems that are caused by it as well, and many of them are the types of human relations problems mentioned here.

Imagine, if you can, a society in which all children receive appropriate guidance, in which all students receive an adequate education, and in which all teenagers receive sufficient moral training and supervision. I find it hard to imagine the existence of such a society without a reduction in the birth rate to a point at which the adults outnumber the children significantly.

It Can't Be Done?

Whenever someone says, "It can't be done," about the only thing that you can be sure of is that the originator of the statement doesn't know how to do "it." If we were to examine the history of most of the consumer products currently on the market, it would probably be found, in the case of most of them, that when their production was first speculated upon, someone said, "It can't be done". And if one could make a similar examination of the origins of most of today's governmental services, it would be found that a similar statement was made somewhere along the way.

The key to getting a lot of the "can't be done" things accomplished is to apply problem-solving skills in an appropriate manner. One of the mistakes that the "can't be done" disciples make is in not clearly understanding the problem that is faced in trying to do "it." Sometimes the problem is not *as great* as they assume it to be. Sometimes the problem is *different* from what they think it is. One of the mistakes that such people make is in either failing to gather adequate new information about the problem or ignoring some of the existing information about the problem. In a lot of cases, the "can't be done" group is ignorant of emerging technologies that make it more likely that it *can* be done. One of the more prominent examples of this is the list of innumerable applications that have been developed for the microchip since it first appeared just a few short years ago. For instance, when I was in college, the calculators which we used were of the mechanical variety, which required that each separate mathematical operation be performed independently of all of the others. If, at that point, someone had speculated about the development of a calculator with which two operations could be performed in sequence, someone probably would have said, "It can't be done." Only a few years later, the invention of the microchip made possible the production of small, hand-held calculators that could perform a lengthy series of operations.

Another example is that of waterproof plywood. When I was young, plywood could not be allowed to get wet, or its layers would almost certainly separate. That characteristic definitely had a limiting effect on productivity in the construction industry. But then the development of waterproof glue changed all of that, so that nowadays all of the plywood that is sold is resistant to moisture-based separation of its layers. A few years before that, someone probably said, "It can't be done," when hearing speculation about the production of non-separating plywood.

The next time that you hear the statement "It can't be done," it might be safest to assume that *it* probably *can* be done, but that the task requires a better understanding of the problem to be confronted, more information related to it, and the emergence of a new technology which probably *will emerge*. And always remember, if someone says, "It can't be done," that may only mean that *they* can't do it.

Rules You Don't Like

Have you ever been confronted by a rule that you didn't like? If not, you're in a very small minority. Perhaps you don't like some rule because you think that it isn't fair, or because it prevents you from doing something that you want to do, or because it forces you to *do* something that you *don't want to do.* One of the prices that we pay for being societal organisms, is that rules are an essential part of our lives. Most rules of society are established for the purpose of enhancing our survival. Lower forms of living things don't consciously establish rules like we do, but they are, nevertheless, subject to the rules of nature, with which their basic instincts dovetail in order to promote survival.

You would have a difficult time finding someone who doesn't resent *some* rule. Furthermore, for every rule that exists, there is probably someone who is trying to figure out a way around it. Not too surprisingly, most of the "ways around it" are illegal, and land the perpetrators in court, and perhaps even in jail. A reaction to distasteful rules that I find not to enter the minds of very many people is that of getting those rules changed. Unfortunately, most people find it easier to evade a rule than to get it altered. But perhaps that situation could be reversed if we offered in the school curriculum a class on how to get rules changed. Some of the more familiar ways of changing rules are petition drives, the initiative process, testifying before local councils and committees, and working on the campaigns of political candidates who also want to get the rules in question revised, and who would be in a position to get them changed through the legislative process.

A great number of people feel that once a rule (law) has been established, it can't be changed or deleted. But we in the United States live in a democracy where that just isn't true. If our democratic process works as theorized, it should be just as easy to get rid of a law that the majority opposes as it is to establish a law that the majority favors. It's mainly a matter of mobilizing the majority to first favor the elimination of the distasteful law, then insist upon its elimination.

It is an inevitable fact of life that we who live in a democracy are going to be faced now and then with rules that we don't like. But seriously consider for a moment the alternative of living in a type of political system where not only is there no opportunity to get a rule changed, but also you automatically go to prison if you get caught violating it, and have no opportunity to appeal your sentence.

The best advice is to not ignore a rule if you don't like it. Instead, take advantage of the fact that you live in a democracy, and work to get it changed. By ignoring it, you undoubtedly tread on the rights of fellow members of your society. By getting it changed, you not only remove it as a barrier to yourself, but also promote the democratic axiom that the majority rules, if it turns out that your opinion of the rule is shared by the majority.

Compromising Situations

Have you ever noticed that the people who are most willing to compromise are those who are about to lose everything? Consider the theoretical example of the child who begs his mother to buy the proverbial candy in the grocery store. She responds that it would spoil his lunch. He begins to cry. She tells him that if he continues to cry, he'll never get candy in the store again. He begins to scream. At this point, she is about to "lose everything;" everyone in the store is contemplating calling the police to investigate child abuse. She then says, "We'll buy this candy, but you'll have to wait until after you have finished your lunch to eat it." That's called a compromise.

Next, let's examine a theoretical example of the common practice of plea bargaining. An arrested criminal starts out by denying any knowledge of the alleged crime and vowing to fight the charges all the way to the Supreme Court. Later, after he is told by his defense attorney that there is a strong chance that he will be convicted and receive a life sentence, he realizes that this is darned close to losing everything. So, at that point, he agrees to compromise, which in this case is called plea bargaining.

At another level, we find many companies that get involved in situations that warrant compromises. A fairly common scenario is that of the company that starts out being highly successful with just a few employees, and which subsequently rapidly expands its staff, inventory, distribution territory, and number of outlets, until it becomes overextended. After creditors proceed to harass them almost continuously, and employees threaten to sue for back pay, and suppliers stop shipping them goods (in other words, when they reach the brink of losing everything), they commit themselves to the ultimate business-compromise, which is to file for bankruptcy.

A final example involves international trade relations. Consider the theoretical country Mergany, which offers for sale a product called a "gizmo." The country of Napaj foresees a threat to their own gizmo industry because the Mergan gizmos are of slightly better quality for the same price. So the Napajese place an embargo on the Mergan gizmos. The Mergans, retaliate by immediately instituting a Mergan embargo on Napajese whatamacallits, thingamabobs, and doohickeys. In short order, the Napajese government realizes that their entire economy (everything?), which is based primarily on the sales of the latter products to Mergany, is about to go down the drain. So, Napaj agrees (compromises?) to permit Mergany to export their gizmos to Napaj as long as they pay a five per cent tariff.

You, as an individual, might find it advisable to educate yourself in the fine art of compromising. That education might come in handy the next time you find yourself in the position of being about to lose everything.

Job Connections

Have you ever heard anyone say that they are confident of finding a job because they have a "connection?" That attitude intermeshes fairly well with the not-always-reliable rule, "It's not what you know, but who you know." Personally, I think that it helps to have a connection primarily if you're *qualified* for the job in question. Under most circumstances, competent personnel directors who have the welfare of their company in mind would be inclined to hire the *most competent* applicant, rather than a friend who is *less competent.* However, it can't be denied that there are cases where friendships have played a greater role in hiring than have qualifications of the applicants. And, that is probably more likely to happen among small companies, wherein the boss/president does the hiring.

I have met a great number of people who have spent much of their lives cultivating connections, while at the same time avoiding development of the job skills that would make them worthwhile employees. Although the latter approach would make them more likely to find a job even without connections, the tales of advantages of "connections" abound nevertheless, and are still believed by a large proportion of the populace.

Of course, it can't be denied that having an extensive network of acquaintances can be an advantage in finding a job *if* you also have the necessary job skills.

When employers are looking for qualified employees, their prospects are limited to those of which they are made aware through various sources. It's probably more likely that the hirer in a *small* company would have a more limited source of applicants' names than the one from a *large* company. Also, the hirer from the small company probably usually has less restrictive rules guiding their choice. But, even in a small company, the company's advantages in hiring the *most qualified* applicant are inescapable.

I'm not discounting the advantage of connections, I'm only attempting to qualify it with a realistic view of the necessity for job skills. One way to improve the probability of your getting a job in the field of your choice is to cultivate friendships with people who work in that field, especially those who are in a position to hire employees. But, in order to *maximize* that probability, you would be well advised to concurrently increase your knowledge and skills in that field. So, while you're seeking out prospective employers to befriend, also seek to read, study, and practice in the field in question.

Just always keep in mind the fact that it usually doesn't help to have connections for a job if the connection doesn't think that you are qualified for the job. And, *what* you know *is* just as important as *who* you know.

Conversationalism

Have you ever noticed that most people are a lot more comfortable talking about topics with which they are *familiar*? That is illustrated by two different conversational types of people that you can observe whenever you get into a setting where small groups are constantly forming and then reforming as conversation is pursued. One type of person that you will notice are the individuals who tend to enter a conversation very little when it is about a topic with which they are unfamiliar. You might think that those people are the shy type who never say very much; however, when the conversation comes around to a topic that they know something about, they go into high gear, and may even dominate for a while. But as soon as that particular topic is exhausted, they revert to the quiet phase immediately.

Another type that one can commonly observe is the incessant talker who also prefers to discuss subjects about which they know a lot, but who talks just enough about every subject that is brought up in the group so that they are in a position to always manage to bring the conversation around to a topic about which they either have extensive opinions or considerable knowledge. You will notice that once a preferred topic of this type is exhausted, they permit only a momentary shift to some other topic before rapidly bringing up another topic on which they have a lot to say.

There is one type of conversationalist that is somewhat rare, but who is the type that we all love to encounter at a conversation-oriented gathering. That is the person who shows an interest in what *we* think or do. They usually initiate a conversation by asking us what *we* think about a particular topic, or what types of activities *we* enjoy, or what *we* have been spending most of our time on lately. They can make just about anyone feel important and welcome at a gathering, and have no difficulty whatsoever in retaining partners-in-talk. You will notice that hardly anyone ever moves away from a conversation with this type of person.

One type of person that is easy to find at most group gatherings is the know-it-all. That's the type that has a poly-verbal response to any topic that is brought up in the group. That type is obviously highly self-impressed with what they know or think. They are also usually *not* extensively impressed by or interested in what anyone else has to say. Whether they are or are not an authority on each of the subjects at hand is not relevant. What matters most is their indifference to the comments of others in the conversational group. My main comment about that type of person is that those who are impressed by all that they know should be even more impressed by all that they *don't* know, which usually tends to be a considerable amount.

Defining The Problem

A lot of human effort is expended in solving peripheral problems rather than basic problems. Here is a theoretical example. Bob is being threatened with termination by his employer because he chronically reports to work about fifteen minutes late. He thinks about how his old jalopy accelerates slowly. He trades-in the jalopy on a new, rapidly-accelerating model, and finds that driving the new car to work saves about five minutes.

Then, on a day off, he explores various alternative routes from home to work, and discovers that by making only a *single* illegal left turn at *one* intersection, he can shift to a route that saves him five more minutes.

Finally, he thinks about the fact that it takes him six minutes just to walk from his parking lot to his desk. By changing to a more expensive, but much closer parking lot, he saves another five minutes.

Voila! Bob has now solved the problem of how to get to work on time. Of course, he has significantly increased his financial obligations through the payments on the new car, the greater number of traffic tickets resulting from speeding and illegal left turns, and a more expensive parking lot. Bob spent all of that time and money solving *peripheral* problems. He totally ignored the *basic* problem, which was that he was getting up fifteen minutes too late every morning. Some of the major problems in the world are treated in just such a peripheral manner. Some examples follow.

> Peripheral problem: not enough money for quality education.
> Basic problem: too high a ratio of school-aged children to tax-paying adults who canpay for the educational system.

> Peripheral problem: the availability of health care is below the level needed by the populace.
> Basic problem: the populace demands more unique, highly specialized procedures than the resources can pay for.

> Peripheral problem: salmon runs depleted because of dams, stream siltation, and pollution.
> Basic problem: the human population is above the level that can be accommodated by the environment.

Perhaps we should add to our school curriculum a class which trains students how to distinguish between peripheral problems and basic problems.

The U.S. Has An Artificial Standard Of Living

E veryone knows that people's standard of living is related to their income. Everyone also
knows that income is related to whether we have a job,
and what kind of job it is. Conventional wisdom tells
us that in order for most people to have well-paying
jobs, the economy has to be "healthy."

What a lot of people don't know, and what conventional wisdom doesn't tell most of us, is that a
government's deficit spending can *artificially* create a
"healthy" economy, and thus artificially create jobs.
The influx of "printing press" money into the economy
of a country *temporarily* stimulates the economy by
giving people more money to spend, thus vitalizing
business in general, and thereby creating more jobs.
This phenomenon feeds on itself: more jobs yield
more money, which in turn causes people to spend
more, which in turn results in the creation of even
more jobs, particularly in the area of *luxury spending.*
Thus, the so-called "healthy" economy spawns all
sorts of luxury industries, including, but not limited
to, the production of things like VCR's, luxury automobiles, fancy speedboats, expansive motorhomes,
cellular phones, and many, many others. You might
find it difficult to identify any young couple who
would agree that a VCR or a cellular phone is a luxury,
as opposed to an essential, but those of us who grew

up during the Great Depression consider a luxury to be just about anything that isn't necessary to keep one alive and healthy.

Well, anyway, to get back to the subject at hand, as long as "printing-press" money flows into the economy, the latter appears to be "healthy." The main problem with the whole process is that the national debt keeps getting bigger and bigger, and the proportion of the tax dollar that is needed just to pay the interest on the national debt keeps expanding. Thus, money that could be spent on things that directly improve the standard of living goes to pay that interest. As the interest on the debt rises, the greater is the stifling effect of the debt on the economy.

In actuality, those countries that enjoy the artificially high standard of living that is created by deficit spending will eventually face the reduction in standard of living to a realistic level. Just take a moment to recall what has happened every time our government has attempted to balance the federal budget: unemployment rates have gone way up, with a resulting drastic reduction in standard of living for all of the people who are out of work. Has anyone ever thought of the fact that perhaps we aren't actually entitled to the artificially high standard of living that we have enjoyed during the years of deficit spending? Is it possible that we should be spending a lower proportion of our income on luxury items? It would be difficult to convince most Americans under the age of 50 of these things.

Financial Security

Financial security is partly a matter of the mind. Among the middle- and upper-class members of our society today, there seems to be a lot of stress about financial security because their parents wanted them to have a better life than they themselves had, and the parents saw to it that the children got it. Now many of those children are adults who can't afford to support their lifestyle expectations.

To explore some theoretical examples, let's look at two different families of four that each has $5,000 to spend on luxuries during the year. The family that spends no more than that can very likely come out of the year feeling financially secure, assuming that other funds have covered all of their *necessities*. They might be satisfied with an automobile camping trip to the Yellowstone Park area, new moderately priced bicycles for the entire family, paying off the balance on a 3-year-old car, renting a waterski boat for use during a week of vacation, and numerous other less expensive luxuries. All of that could easily be covered by the available $5,000.

Then consider the other family of four, which also has $5,000 to spend on luxuries, but who feel the need to indulge themselves far beyond the level of the first family that was discussed. Television advertising convinces them that they deserve two weeks in Hawaii. They also purchase top-of-the-line mountain bikes for every member of the family. TV commercials also cause them to feel that almost every family in America owns a racy speedboat, so they get one. And peer pressure from their many "Jones" friends who own BMW, Mercedes, and Porsche automobiles stimulates them to get a similar type of car in order to keep up. All of those purchases in their one-year total of luxury items come with a price tag of about $75,000, which they of course don't have on hand. But, being people "of means", they do have credit cards and the availability of bank credit, so they have no difficulty in covering their costs.

Now let's examine the financial security of the two families. Let's assume that both families started with no debts other than their house payment and car payment. The family which was discussed first has actually reduced its overall debt by paying off the balance on the car and by not spending any more on luxuries than their available funds warranted. The family which was discussed second has increased their indebtedness by about $70,000, and now has to face the reality of paying that off. Which family do you think has the greater feelings of financial security? The difference in their relative feelings of security would be magnified, of course, if the income-earners in both households lost their jobs.

Perhaps the statement that financial security is mainly a matter of the mind should be supplemented with the following: "If you don't mind living without things that you can't afford, it is much easier to have a feeling of financial security."

Free Health Care For All

We can afford free health care for everyone on earth. In fact, we can hardly afford not to provide everyone with free health care. When I make this statement, I am keeping in mind the fact that a major component of health care should be of the preventive type. When costs of preventive health care are compared with the costs of the treatment of preventable infirmities, the result shows that the investment in the preventive type makes sense. And of course, preventable health problems comprise a large proportion of the total bulk of health problems.

Then what about non-preventable health problems, such as those which are inevitable because they result from the aging process in humans? Can we justify, on a purely financial basis, the provision of free care for those kinds of problems? That justification may not prove to be so easy as the one already discussed. In making an attempt to do it, one thing we should do is to consider the vast amount of human financial wealth from private sources that is already being expended on such care. If all of that money were to go into a central fund for providing free health care for all, it would significantly reduce the balance needed from other sources. One topic that is inescapable from this type of discussion is the question of health-care rationing. It seems highly unlikely that the world financial situation will ever permit free coverage for every type of medical condition. The possibility of free health care for all is much more likely in a scenario wherein only *basic* health care is covered, and highly specialized or outrageously expensive treatment or medical procedures would not be paid for by the government.

Engaging in the current debate about the advisability of governmentally sponsored health care are many who are effectively blocking the designing of a free health care system because of their unwillingness to eliminate *any* types of medical problems from the list of those to be covered. I think that it is safe to say that our government could easily provide free health care for all if governmental coverage were denied for about a couple of dozen of the most expensive medical procedures that have been developed. One of the choices that we may face is that between free *basic* health care coverage for *all* and the current situation in which the availability of health care is closely correlated with level of income or *employers'* ability to provide coverage. Under the existing circumstances, even basic health care is not available to a sizeable proportion of the population.

Perhaps the theory of free health care for all can be implemented if we include only *basic* health care. An acceptable compromise might be to provide such health care free for everyone, and to permit those who can afford to pay for the more highly specialized forms of treatment to do so.

Statisticians And Gamblers

One thing that statisticians and gamblers have in common is that they both deal extensively with the field of probability, which is commonly called "the odds." But, do you know the main *difference* between statisticians and gamblers? Well, it is that statisticians usually use the odds wisely to their advantage, whereas gamblers consistently try to beat the odds. Most tried and true statisticians would seldom invest in any enterprise that had less than a chance of 50 per cent of returning an amount *equal to* their original investment. But, most gamblers routinely put money into operations that have a much smaller chance than that of returning their investment.

One of the most common forms of gambling known to man is the slot machine. What most slot-machine players may not know is that almost all slot machines are set in such a manner that the odds favor the house. Another way of putting it is that the chances of the player getting back at least equal money is less than 50 per cent

I have a friend who resides in Las Vegas, but who denies vehemently that he is a gambler. He rarely plays any games or puts money into any operation that provides less than 50/50 odds. Therefore, he restricts his "gambling" activities to things like black-jack, horse-race betting, and baseball betting. All of those are activities with respect to which he has developed a level of expertise that assures him of better than 50/50 odds. He never plays some of the more popular games like slot machines or keno because skill cannot change the odds of those games to favor the player.

I personally apply the use of the odds to my daily life in many ways. One of the more unusual ways is my approach to fishing for salmon. Although most of my friends consider me to be a highly devoted fisherman because I fish for salmon at least 60 days a year, most of them don't realize that I never go fishing unless the chance of catching a salmon is at least 50 per cent. I arrange that primarily by applying my knowledge of the characteristics of migratory and feeding habits of the fish.

I don't mean to say that statisticians never gamble. Many statisticians are inveterate gamblers despite their understanding of probability, mainly because of the entertainment value of the gambling. There is a certain degree of enjoyment that is derived by most people when they know that they have *any* chance of winning in a gambling situation, even if it is a very small chance. That may explain why there are so many people who buy state lottery tickets in spite of the fact that their chances of winning on any individual ticket are only one in several million.

Getting back to the original premise of this discussion, it's a matter of fact that intelligence tells us to use the odds wisely, but the gambling instinct tells us to try to beat the odds.

Gamete Screening

You may know that the term "gamete" is used to denote reproductive cells like eggs and sperms. Those gametes carry coded genetic information that determines the eventual characteristics of the mature individuals that result from the union of the egg and sperm. That coded information is present in entities to which we commonly refer by the name "gene." Science has demonstrated that if a gene contains defective information, its passage to the fertilized egg, or zygote, and hence, through cell reproduction, to the mature individual, can result in abnormal physical or mental characteristics in that individual. Science has shown us that many anomalistic characteristics in human beings are the result of the passage of defective genes from parents to offspring through the gametes. And, something that is undeniable is that many of those characteristics not only result in pain or suffering for those individuals that possess them, but that they can also cause physical, emotional, and financial stress for relatives and friends, or for society as a whole.

If we are interested in reducing the *total* level of misery for the *total* human population, one thing that we might consider is to reduce the abundance of defective genes in the human population by screening out those gametes that carry them. Currently, to my knowledge, the technology for achieving that does not exist. However, genetic screening of early-stage

human *embryos* has been accomplished by rer
and analyzing a single cell from embryos as .....
pletely developed as the eight-cell stage. In at least
one case, this method of screening has been used to
select an embryo for implantation in the uterus of a
prospective mother. I assume that any non-selected
embryos involved in that process were destroyed.

Although embryo-screening could achieve some
of the same genetic goals as gamete-screening, it has
one major flaw, which is that it is looked upon as
abortion by most pro-life groups. The majority of the
members of such groups interpret the beginning of
human life to be conception, the union of the egg and
sperm, and any interference with the survival of the
organism beyond that point is considered to be abortion, which, of course, a significant proportion of the
human population opposes.

Well, conceivably that objection could be avoided
through gamete-screening, or the selection and rejection of eggs and sperms *prior to* their union. Undoubtedly, the process of screening gametes for gene defects would be opposed by some people for a variety
of reasons. The availability of that technology could
raise all sorts of ethical questions, a major one being
that of defining "defective" to the satisfaction of the
majority of the human population. The process of
developing a definition that would be applied to gene
selection or rejection is sure to sound a multitude of
religious and political alarm bells.

A Guaranteed Annual Income

Every time I have observed the concept of a guaranteed annual income to be promoted by a member of the executive or legislative branches of our federal government, there have been detractors who have claimed that the availability of such a benefit would destroy the work ethic of our populace. What those detractors have apparently overlooked, however, is the fact that their contention is based upon the doubtful assumption that a guaranteed annual income would be set at a level that would satisfy an unacceptably high proportion of the populace.

The debate about the advisability and practicability of a guaranteed annual income involves several highly variable factors, including the level of purchasing power to be represented by the guaranteed income, the amount of effort toward public service and the like that would have to be expended in return for the guaranteed income, and the proportion of income that the supporting citizenry would have to pay in taxes in order to implement such a concept. It is conceivable that a combination of levels of these factors could be established that would make the total package acceptable to the vast majority of voters.

Although the opponents of the idea of a guaranteed annual income might find it difficult to imagine, the societal benefits of such a program could be extensive. One major advantage could be that in many families the parents might have to spend less time in earning money for basic needs, and could spend more time on proper upbringing of the children. Another would be the benefit of students being able to spend more time studying and less time working for money to provide for basic needs.

The possibility of a guaranteed annual income becoming a reality might increase if we could develop a very inexpensive source of energy, something other than the current costly sources such as fossil fuels and hydroelectricity. Because the bulk of the costs involved with supplying a minimal but reasonable standard of living are represented by the cost of energy, the availability of very inexpensive energy could improve that standard. In conjunction with the concept of a guaranteed annual income, perhaps the guarantee could come in the form of an energy allowance that could be either used by the recipient or sold in order to obtain funds to be used for other needs.

As far as the matter of the destruction of the work ethic is concerned, it would be essential to set the level of the guaranteed income at that at which only a very small proportion of the population would be satisfied with, and which would thus leave the majority with a stimulus for working and earning even more money.

The Real Reason For The High Cost Of Health Care

I am continually perplexed by the fact that the vast majority of the healthcare experts who are quoted in the media appear to ignore the primary reason for the high cost of health care. The main villains that are pointed out by most universal healthcare advocates are the doctors who are allegedly charging excessive fees for their services. Those doctors in turn refer primarily to the high cost of malpractice insurance as the reason for their high fees and low profits.

Rarely do I see any reference to what I consider to be the real reason for the high cost of health care. That is the populace's insistence on the availability of relatively new and very expensive medical procedures at the expense of the government or insurance companies or hospitals. Some of the medical procedures of which I speak are heart/lung transplants, liver transplants, and gene therapy, all of them forms of treatment that we lived (or died?) without just a few short years ago. Only a very subtle reference to the problem of the demand for these expensive services has been made, and it has come in the form of the use of the phrase "rationed health care". However, that phrase has been treated with such ambiguity in the press, that one can only guess that users of the phrase might be thinking of limiting the availability of some of the more expensive, rare forms of medical treatment.

It is a given fact that the current level of government and insurance company financial resources for health care cannot possibly pay for all of the care that is demanded by the public. Therefore, the question that arises is, "Do we raise more money through increased health insurance premiums and increased taxes in order to pay for all of the health care that is demanded, or do some of the medically needy go without the health care that they demand?" I think that most people would agree that there is a limit to how high a level of insurance premiums the public can pay, or how much tax they can pay. So the question becomes one of at what point we should limit health care in order to stay within the boundaries of the financial resources that are available for paying for it. As far as I can tell, that question has been almost completely ignored during the current debate over health care. Instead of blaming the doctors or the malpractice lawyers for the high cost of health care, let's focus on the real culprits, who are the sizeable proportion of the U.S. population who demand more subsidized, highly specialized health care than *their* country can afford.

The Stability Of The AIDS Virus

When the existence of the HIV virus which causes AIDS was originally recognized, its presence appeared to be primarily in homosexual men and intravenous drug users. About that time, it was proclaimed by numerous religious conservatives that AIDS was God's way of punishing sinners. Since then, AIDS has become relatively common among non-sinners, like hemophiliacs and even heterosexuals. Well, if God's intent was to punish sinners through the spread of the HIV virus, God made a grave mistake by underestimating the ability of the virus to migrate far beyond the intended limits.

In the early years of the AIDS epidemic, the term "at-risk group" was used in reference to the homosexual males and the intravenous drug users among whom it most frequently was manifested. But, now AIDS is becoming so common among groups who are not considered to be "at-risk," that the term has become somewhat meaningless. Or, another way of putting it would be to say that anyone who receives a body fluid or potential virus-containing medium of any type from any other person is "at-risk." That definition would include a significant proportion of the population.

A very frightening possibility that I have never heard discussed in any of the media reports on the HIV virus is that of its mutating into a form that could be spread by casual contact, in much the same way

94

that influenza viruses are now spread. The fact that many viruses do undergo mutations is indisputable. It is common knowledge, for example, that influenza viruses mutate almost annually into new varieties. At least that is given as the reason why new types of flu vaccines have to be developed. Well, despite the availability of flu vaccines to much of the industrialized world, flu epidemics occur in the industrialized nations almost every year. Fortunately, most flu victims' bodies are able to overcome the invading flu virus within a few days, and return to normal fairly rapidly. However, to this point, no AIDS victim has ever demonstrated the ability overcome the HIV virus.

In the initial stages of the AIDS epidemic, the term "at-risk" seemed appropriate because it was assumed that the HIV virus could be contracted only by people who engaged in specific types of unusual and generally unacceptable behaviors. But that outlook has already changed significantly.

Looking further down the road, imagine how the HIV virus could decimate the human population if it mutated into a form that could be spread by casual contact in the way that flu is spread. The thought of such a scenario should deter us from thinking of AIDS as the problem of only certain "at-risk" groups, and should spur us on to putting more of our energy and funds into the development of AIDS-prevention technology.

On Being Ignorant

It is very doubtful that there is any person any where in the world who is not ignorant about *some* subject. Being ignorant means not knowing something that is known by at least one other person. Or, more likely, it means not knowing something that is known by *many other people*. The degree of ignorance of people ranges from those who are ignorant about almost every subject, to those who are ignorant about very few subjects. But even the most intelligent people in the world are not totally immune to ignorance. I think that it's safe to say that everyone who is an expert in some field is ignorant in at least one other field. Many of us commonly make the mistake of assuming that an "expert" who is presented to us has expertise in almost all fields of study.

I also think that it's safe to say that people who have a low degree of ignorance generally have a better self-image than those who have a high degree of ignorance. If you have ever come out of a meeting or other group situation in which you were made to realize that you knew relatively little about the subject under discussion, you know what I mean. If the realization of that ignorance didn't make your self-esteem waiver just a little bit, you're probably in a small minority. And, if you have never had such an experience resulting from a group meeting, you're probably in an even smaller minority, or you haven't attended a very great variety of meetings.

Most of us feel at least slightly chagrined about any ignorance of which we are found to be guilty, but ignorance is much less shameful if we are constantly trying to overcome it. One of the greatest confidence-building activities that has ever existed is the accumulation of knowledge by the individual. There is a common statement that says, "Knowledge is power," but there is a parallel statement that could say, "Knowledge is a confidence-builder." If people want their children to have a good self-image, one way to help build it is to assist the children in acquiring knowledge. That should prove to be much more effective than the very common parenting technique of giving the child status symbols, which only help the self-image temporarily and artificially. Gifts of fancy pro-team sweatshirts, expensive bicycles, the "in" athletic shoes, or other symbols can give only a fleeting sense of self-worth.

During my many years of teaching, I observed the following phenomenon: the existence of a high level of confidence among those students who had abundant knowledge, and the existence of a lack of self-assurance among those students who had relatively meager knowledge. One of the greater rewards of teaching was observing the growth in confidence that students exhibited as they accumulated knowledge.

So, if you want to help your children build self-confidence, help them to identify and implement ways of overcoming the ignorance that so commonly accompanies youth and immaturity.

97

Creative Thinking

M ost people allow their thinking to be limited by the status quo. They tend to think within the boundaries of how things are, rather than to let their thinking explore outside those boundaries, in the realm of how things *could be.*

One example which comes to mind in this regard is from my early years. When I was a child, the trimming of the parts of the lawn where the lawnmower couldn't reach was done with what would now be considered to be a very primitive type of grass shears. They consisted of a single piece of steel, bent into a V-form, with the two points of the "V" forged into the flat shape of blades. The blades had to be controlled with very precise and tedious motions of the wrists and fingers; that process got *very* tiresome *very* fast!

As I was growing up, various inventors came up with improvements to the basic grass shears. One was the change to a two-*piece* design, which operated much like scissors. Later, someone came up with the idea of a four-piece design that permitted the operator to use a vertical squeezing action of the fingers instead of the traditional horizontal action.

Then, when I was middle-aged, someone developed an idea that revolutionized grass-trimming because it went beyond the limited thinking about the shears type. It involved the extension of nylon strings from a whirling disc operated by a small motor, and came under the general classification "string-trimmer."

A critical point that I want to emphasize here is that for years the thinking about grass-trimmer design was apparently limited to the status quo: the shears type.

Numerous examples of how creative thinking has led us away from the status quo, and toward new methods and materials, can be found in our daily lives. Some of them are the following: teaching through cooperative learning; friction activated chemical handwarmers; tubeless automobile tires; man-made fibers like nylon and Dacron; and home equity credit lines. A key element which is common to all of the foregoing developments is that for years the thinking about improvements in their predecessors was limited to minor improvements, within the boundaries of the status quo.

It is very likely that these inventions would never have been developed without concurrent development of new technologies. But, the important thing to remember is that the paths of the creative minds of the inventors, who allowed their thinking to stray outside the status quo, crossed the paths of emerging technologies at an opportune time.

National Security Through Isolationism Or Samaritanism?

During most of the twentieth century, the United States has been looked upon by the majority of the other countries of the world as the primary defender of democracy and human rights. In that role, we sent our armed forces to Europe, the South Pacific, Asia, and the Middle East. We justified our forays into foreign lands by claiming that they were an essential part of our national security measures. The feeling generally was that if we did not intercede in the crises experienced by those nations which tended to be aligned with us, successes by villainous rebel leaders in those nations or capture of those nations by external enemies would threaten our national security by allowing a domino effect which could eventually spread to our own continent.

It should be pointed out that at the time of those armed interventions by the United States in other parts of the world, we were considered both by ourselves and by others to be a rich nation that could afford such ventures. In reality, for the most part, we were financing those interventions through deficit spending. While we were conquering the rebel and enemy leaders in other parts of the world, we were permitting a more insidious and subtle foe to develop within our borders; that was national debt. We were also witnessing in our country a population expansion which has led to increased crime and decreased quality of education, both of which are somewhat related to increased use of drugs, and all three of which could be more threatening to our national security than any external armed threat.

In order to serve as the primary defender of democracy and human rights in the world, a country must have both financial wealth and moral wealth. But both of those types of wealth have declined drastically during the past few years, to the point that the threat of our own internal instability is more of a danger than external aggression. Financial statistics prove that we are definitely no longer a monetarily wealthy nation, but that we are, instead ,the greatest debtor nation in the world. And crime statistics suggest that we may also no longer be a morally wealthy country.

So, perhaps it is time that we reduce the emphasis on our role as worldwide Good Samaritans, and increase the emphasis on rebuilding our own financial and moral wealth. The limits of our resources require that we make such a choice, that we shift the utilization of those resources *away from* the defense of democracy abroad, and *toward* the reinforcement of democracy within our own borders. If we don't do that, I see a great likelihood that our government will eventually be toppled from *within*, something that has, to this point, not been accomplished by *external* forces.

The Lemming Mentality

Have you heard about the lemmings? They are those furry little creatures which live in Scandinavia, and which leap off cliffs and into the sea by the hundreds of thousands. They also die from that maneuver by the hundreds of thousands. Scientists who have studied the lemmings have not come up with a definitive explanation for the phenomenon, but they suspect that the leaders of the movement have an instinctive desire to do such leaping, and then the rest of the horde follows along just because "everybody else is doing it." That inclination gives rise to the phrase "lemming mentality." It also results in endangerment of the lemming as a species.

Well, it isn't only lemmings that have a lemming mentality. You can witness it almost everyday in the human population, too, where it is usually more subtle than jumping off cliffs. It probably reaches its peak among American teenagers. An extremely common illustration of teenage lemming mentality occurs when it comes to their reacting to the latest "cool" band. Have you ever noticed how the promoters of such bands never have any difficulty filling the largest arena around? Do you think that is because all of those teenagers can't live without that band's music? Don't kid yourself: they're all going just because *everybody else is going!*

Some more evidence of the lemming mentality in teenagers is their slavish but fickle response to teen fashions. A type of clothing can be all the rage among the teenage population one week, but forgotten and replaced by a new fad the next week. The quickest way to riches is to develop a product that no teenager could live without, even if it's only because they think that none of the other teenagers could live without it either.

Adults shouldn't feel smug about this, though. Examples of the lemming mentality are common among the adult population, too. For example, when someone purchased that last pair of "hot" athletic shoes, do you think that it was because they were the best bargain? the most medically correct for their feet? the most durable material? I doubt it. More than likely, it was because all of their friends were buying them, too.

Some of the objects of the lemming mentality in adult humans include 4-wheel-drive vehicles, special brands of clothing, socially correct brands of sports implements, and hairstyles. All of those things can also be called "status symbols." A good definition of a status symbol would be "something that you want because you think that its possession by you will raise your status in the opinion of your friends." That definition dovetails fairly well with the definition of "lemming mentality."

The Reality Of Credit Spending

C redit spending should be outlawed! It has
created a financial strangle-hold on America.
Our economy is so thoroughly addicted to credit spending,
that the cessation of that phenomenon would cause
budgetary withdrawal symptoms that would make
those of a habit-kicking heroin junkie seem minuscule. The principal financial drug for the credit-rich
and cash-poor is, of course, the credit card. It is one
of the main reasons why the personal debt load of the
average citizen of the United States is greater than
that of the people in any other country of the world.
The family financial health in this country is jeopar-
dized by the coupling of the easy purchasing power
of the credit card with the fact that TV advertising
leads us to believe that every person in the world is
entitled to an annual trip to a sunny vacation resort,
home-delivered pizza for every dinner, a luxurious
motor home, a sexy speedboat, the latest in clothing
fashions, and the list goes on and on.

At the governmental level, credit spending goes
by the aliases "deficit spending" and "long-term bond
levies." The greatest perpetrator of deficit spending
on earth is, naturally, the United States government.
And look at the trouble that has gotten us into. We
now spend an outrageous proportion of every tax
dollar just to pay the *interest* on the national debt.
Think for a minute about what we could do if that
amount were available to pay for budget items on a

cash basis! For one thing, we could afford to assure every person in the country a decent minimum standard of living!

The one big advantage of credit spending is that you can live it up *now* (even though you can't afford it). Two big disadvantages are: you have to pay it back eventually or suffer dire consequences, and you have to pay the interest on the debt in the meantime.

Our addiction to credit spending is much like being hooked on drugs. The more long lasting and extensive it becomes, the more severe the withdrawal symptoms will be if we ever try to kick it. Some economists express the credit spending problem in a different way. They liken it to a balloon that is being inflated by the credit spending. The balloon is destined to burst at some point in time, and the larger it inflates, the bigger the bang is going to be.

Experts And Ignorance

It would behoove everyone to be aware of the fact that every person who is an expert in some field is ignorant in some other field. But, have you ever noticed how many manufacturers employ famous people to attest to the quality of products that are totally unrelated to the respective fields of expertise? And have you observed that many stars of stage, screen, and sports venture into business and politics on the assumption that their fame will automatically bring them success in fields of endeavor other than those for which they originally became well known? Those activities often spring from the notion that a person who is an expert on one topic is also an expert on most other topics. However, it is undeniable that the opposite is true.

One of the best examples available would be that of Albert Einstein, who is generally accepted as one of the top intellectuals of all time. It can't be denied that old Al' knew a lot about relativity, gravity, electromagnetism, and the like. However, how much do you think that he knew about repairing a broken-down automobile engine, the best bass lures, or the best janitorial procedures for cleaning the floor of a high school? The answer is, "Probably not much," because Einstein was just as subject as the rest of us are to the axiom in question here. It would probably be safe to say that old Al' could have readily picked up the necessary knowledge to become exceedingly qualified on those topics if he had put his mind to it. But, he just never got interested in them, as far as I know. Einstein is an excellent example of the fact that knowledge and skill are not a function of intellect alone, but also require interest and application in most cases.

Actually, expertise in one field could very well cause dangerous overconfidence in some other field in which a person is relatively ignorant. For example, a leading rocket scientists could create limitless confusion and havoc by straying into an unfamiliar field like international relations. That is not to say, however, that it is impossible for a rocket scientist to be adequately familiar with the arena of international relations to contribute significantly to the latter.

If you have never been witness to the phenomenon of the "expert" bungling their way through a unfamiliar field, you have missed a very entertaining situation. It occurs occasionally during TV interviews on talk shows. Of course, your average one-field intellect can usually disguise the fact that they are "talking through their hat." It takes an alert viewer to distinguish this.

The wandering of one-field experts into areas of incompetency could lead to an offshoot to the Peter Principle. As you may know, that principle states that every person will eventually rise to his level of incompetence. The offshoot, which I will call "The Hansler Principle," states that every expert who is not cautious will eventually manage to get himself mired down in a topic about which he is relatively ignorant. That is an important principle for you to remember if you ever find yourself regarded as an "expert."

Being Competitive

There is a lot of talk among politicians these days that indicates that America should be more competitive for world markets, and Americans should be more competitive for jobs. The trouble with that concept is that being competitive implies that there have to be losers. Competition is all right in sports, where the losing team can simply shrug off their loss and reorganize for the next game; but when we're talking about someone, somewhere losing a job, the scenario gets serious, especially if we're the someone. Being the loser in an athletic contest, where what is lost is usually merely some superficial pride, is very different from losing in economic competition, where one may never recover from the financial loss. The concept that there have to be winners and losers when it comes to competing for jobs is a bit archaic, considering that (1) the world has shrunk significantly in recent years because of improved transportation and communications systems, and (2) human beings have the capacity for assuring everyone on earth the *opportunity* for a high standard of living.

We often hear of the need for assuring every American an opportunity to attain the "American Dream." Well, how about setting the goal of assuring every citizen of the world a chance of attaining the "American Dream." Perhaps we should call it the "Universal Dream." Instead of thinking in terms of country-by-country economies, we should be thinking in terms of a global economy, where every country is interdependent with all of the others. Even more important, we should be thinking in terms of a global minimum standard of living. The human race has the intellectual, scientific, and technological capacity for making available the opportunity for the "Universal Dream" for everyone in every country all over the earth.

The primary, most basic problem that this goal faces is that there are too many people competing for the basic necessities of life on this planet. The most utterly basic of all those necessities isn't food or water, but is, instead, inexpensive energy, which could be used to make all of the other necessities available in very adequate amounts for everyone. The availability of cheap energy could assure a sub-maximum human population a much higher standard of living than the average human being now experiences.

Instead of competing for world markets and jobs, which inevitably will lead to just about as many losers as winners, we should proceed to create a world situation that gives everyone the opportunity for attaining the "American/Universal Dream." But, without a reduced human world population and abundant, inexpensive energy, it will probably never happen.

The Health Of Our Economy

Our economy is dependent on deficit spending. The only time the United States seems to have a "healthy" economy is when it is spending more money that it is taking in. That process adds, of course, to the national debt, which harms us all financially in a very subtle, insidious way. If one seriously considers the fact that a large portion of every tax dollar is used just to pay off the interest on the national debt, the true effect of our ever-increasing national debt comes more clearly into focus. However, any consideration of the effect of the national debt upon our national standard of living seems to be overshadowed in most people's minds by consideration of the effect that the elimination of their own favorite government handouts would have on their personal standard of living.

I consider it to be highly unlikely that the American public will ever support elimination of deficit spending, because of the long list of amenities that the average person would have to give up. Just think for a minute of all of the government services which you receive, but which you would have to do without if the government ceased deficit spending. Cessation of deficit spending would cause an economic reaction similar to the withdrawal that drug addicts go through when they try to kick their drug habit. In actuality, we the American people are addicted to deficit spending, and if we tried to kick our spending habit, we would suffer the greatest set of withdrawal symptoms ever witnessed.

Well, if deficit spending by the federal government has such a stimulating effect on our economy, why not adopt it as a routine part of our budgeting process? The reasons for that are two-fold. First, if we continued to increase the national debt , we would undoubtedly eventually get to a point where its effects, which are not now very noticeable upon our standard of living, would become *extremely* noticeable. Second, we would eventually discover that the United States was not owned by its people, but was, instead, owned by the people who hold the government bonds, and that includes large numbers of rich foreigners.

Of course, deficit spending isn't only a governmental process. It is also practiced by a major percentage of individual Americans, largely in the form of outstanding balances on loans and credit cards. The same sort of artificially stimulating effect that governmental deficit spending has on the national economy is evident in regard to personal economy as a result of a person living on credit, but, of course, it is much more obvious to the individual that the credit spending can't go on forever.

I may be wrong, but I doubt that the deficit spending machine is one that can go on for very long without a major breakdown.

We May Have Already Damaged The Environment Irreversibly

A lmost every day we see, in the news media, reports of damage to our environment. In almost all of the cases, the environmental damage is caused by human activities. Environmentalists work constantly to develop ways to modify human activities so that those activities do less harm to the environment. One example of how they have succeeded is the limiting or prohibiting of woodburning stoves and outdoor burning in order to lower the introduction of smoke into the air. Another is the practice of requiring settling basins for the run-off from all construction projects where the surface of the earth is disturbed. That helps to prevent siltation of fish-spawning streams, among other things. There are many other notable examples of successes by environmentalists in regard to altering the results of human activities so that the effects on the environment are minimized.

There are, however, *some* human activities that can never be eliminated entirely, and which are destined to forever have *some* negative effects on the environment. They include, among others, the need for obtaining food, the need for shelter, and the elimination of human waste products. Each of those activities had relatively insignificant negative effects on the environment during the period of human existence when the population was small, but now that the human population has increased tremendously, they all have very noticeable negative effects. All three of those activities have significant effects upon either the quality of the atmosphere or the quality of our bodies of water. Some of the effects upon the atmosphere have been fairly obvious, such as the highly polluted air in the major urban areas of the world. One of the noticeable effects on our bodies of water has been widespread deaths of aquatic animal life.

Many scientists have been warning us about what could happen if we continue to pollute the air and the water in the way that we have been doing, but up to this point, I am not aware that *any* scientist has suggested that we may have *already* damaged those parts of the environment to a point that the damage is *irreversible,* and to the point that it could result in destruction of human life, either directly or indirectly. Who is to say that we haven't already damaged the atmosphere to the point where plant life will eventually die out. Of course, without plant life we can't survive, because we need the oxygen that the plant life produces. And, who is to say that we haven't already damaged the oceans to the extent that aquatic life will eventually die out, and thus our major source of food will be eliminated.

Let's hope that our concern about the environment hasn't arrived too late!

Why There Should Be Free K-16 Public Education

I am convinced that the government should make available to every intellectually qualified individual a free kindergarten through college education. Naturally, the average person's initial reaction to this idea will be extremely negative, based primarily on the inferred cost of such a program. Well, some expensive things are bargains, particularly when they hold the promise of returning to the investor the cost of the investment many times over. And that would be true of the free K-16 education.

Actually, most governments already provide a free K-12 education for their citizens, so it isn't as though the entire K-16 program is a new idea. I'm simply suggesting the addition of four more years. They don't have to be college years. They could be any kind of education that gave the student further preparation for a productive life in our society.

To borrow a statement from the United Negro College Fund, "A mind is a terrible thing to waste!" To take it a step further, a mind is a wonderful thing to nurture to its maximum capacity. And that is what could be enhanced by the additional four years of free education.

Let's take a look at what would be gained by offering the additional four years:

1. A large percentage of students, who otherwise

would have to dilute their attention to studies by working part-time to pay for their education, could devote their full energies to the demands of their educational program.
2. Many people who have to terminate their formal education upon completion of high school could, instead, attend for the additional four years.
3. The pool of workers that would be available to business, industry, and all other types of skilled-labor employers would have a significantly higher level of skills than they now have.
4. The more highly skilled work force would be a stimulus to the economy, because it would:
   a. require less government assistance than a low skilled work force.
   b. be more productive than a low-skilled work force.
   c. pay more taxes back to the government.

In addition to the above-named advantages, a well-educated population would be more likely to support, defend, and promote the principles of democracy.

Homelessness

We should be providing every citizen with a guaranteed minimum standard of living! There is adequate technology and sufficient wealth in the world to permit us to make that an inalienable benefit. I'm talking here about only the very basic necessities and comforts of life, things that just about everyone, including the most dyed-in-the-wool conservatives, would agree upon. I mean things like three well balanced meals a day; a warm, dry place with a comfortable bed to sleep at night; perhaps even the opportunity to take a shower once a day.

I must say that I am troubled to find that even some of my most charitable friends are reluctant to hand out anything free to the unfortunate. They feel that handouts create a chronic welfare group. But, I don't think that their feeling applies to the basic minimums that I have in mind. I can't believe that a significant percentage of people would be satisfied to live permanently with the kind of standard of living that I am suggesting, if they had the ability to better their lot by getting a paying job. The minimum offering that I envision would be set up much like a prison, and would be run in military style, with sufficiently austere accommodations and sufficiently strict rules to discourage anyone from wanting to reside in those accomodations any longer than the minimum time it would take to get back on their feet financially. However, the main difference between the proposed facil-

116

ity and a prison would be that the residents would be free to come and go as they wished. Currently up-to-date prison-types of facilities, with a few minor modifications, would seem to be suitable for the accomodations that I have in mind. We would want them to be fairly indestructible (as most prison accomodations are), and sufficiently secure to prevent residents from harming other residents or their property.

The statistics on the homeless and poverty-stricken indicate that our society has a definite need for the kind of safety net that I advocate here, in order to help those people who are temporarily down and out.

One of my more charitable, yet ideologically resistant friends made a useful suggestion that he said would make the general idea acceptable to him. He proposed that the free room and board be coordinated with requirements for some type of minimum constructive activity on the part of able-bodied residents. That could include, among other things, job training or public service. Of course, those who had disabling problems could be at least partially exempted from such requirements.

If you are resistant to this idea of providing a minimum standard of living for everyone, imagine for a moment that all of your net worth has just been wiped out by some physical or financial disaster. Under those circumstances, even you might think that the offering of a free minimum standard of living was a pretty good idea!

Living Your Life

I once read the following quotation: "Live your life as if each day is your last, but also as if you will live forever." Over the years since I read it, it has made more and more sense to me. I have thought about some of the things that we would do if this day were our last.

Wouldn't we tell our loved ones how much we really loved them, even though most of us rarely seem to get around to doing it under normal circumstances?

Wouldn't we attempt to do something to make sure that we left the earth a better place than when we arrived? And it wouldn't have to be heroics, only small but meaningful deeds.

Wouldn't we try to eliminate any enmity which anyone might feel toward us, and to eliminate the reasons for that enmity as much as possible? It would seem such a shame to leave this world knowing that anyone despised us dreadfully, or even resented us in a minor way.

Wouldn't we do whatever we could do in our short remaining time to reduce human misery? Perhaps we couldn't do much toward this task in the space of one day, but just giving some of our remaining food to the starving or comforting the pain-wracked elderly would help.

Wouldn't we do whatever we could to assure perpetuation of our species? Because this is one of the primary purposes of all other living species, it is very likely that contributing something significant toward its accomplishment would be important.

Next, let's examine what changes we would make in our daily lives if we thought that we were going to live forever. We almost certainly would avoid doing anything that could possibly come back to haunt us in later life. For example, wouldn't we try to avoid committing any kind of crime? When the average criminal makes the statement, "They'll never catch me," doesn't he mean "in the span of the normal human life?"

Wouldn't we try to make sure that we stayed in good health, so that we could *enjoy* our extended life? An eternal life certainly would be much less enjoyable if we suffered emphysema because of smoking, or liver damage because of drinking, or quadriplegism because we crashed our motorcycle and weren't wearing a helmet.

And, actually, wouldn't we work harder on some of the same goals that we would identify if this day were our last? Wouldn't we work to make the earth a better place if we were destined to spend eternity on it? Wouldn't we try to avoid arousing the enmity of those with whom we had to come into frequent contact if we were going to have to live with them forever?

The next time you're contemplating either *doing* something or *not doing* something else, think about its significance to your life if you had only one day to live, but also if you were going to live forever.

The Ultimate Test

Of all of the human tasks that warrant the development of a set of preparatory skills, probably none is more critical than that of being a parent. Ironically, parenting is one of the few skill-demanding endeavors for which there is no test of skills that must be passed before embarking on the task. We're all familiar with the multitude of tests which must be passed before one may pursue various vocational, educational, and recreational activities. For example, there are the bar exam for a law degree, the oral exams for a PhD degree, the SAT tests for entrance into college, the CAB test for prospective operators of radio-controlled model airplanes, and the Cosmetology Board Exam for those wishing to pursue a career as a cosmetologist.

Unfortunately, the primary task which the vast majority of human beings end up undertaking requires no prior test of skills. It is sad to realize that a human being with absolutely no skill in child-upbringing can become a parent. It certainly isn't because parenting skills aren't important. Actually, the more one learns about such skills, the more important they seem to be. The more books and magazines that one reads about parenting skills, the more that one realizes the magnitude of the task of proper parenting. In fact, we might make great strides toward causing post-puberty human beings to delay pregnancy if we would just require every pre-puberty individual to read at least one of the leading books on parenting.

If we were not trying to perpetuate a civilized society, parenting skills might not be so consequential. But, an appropriate level of skill in bringing up children is essential if we want the majority of our citizens to believe in democracy and to be able to successfully participate in it. Could it be that the recent deterioration of our society, as indicated by things such as crime statistics and poverty, is related to the increasingly common phenomenon of "children having children?" By the former, I mean socially immature, inadequately educated young people, who not only have no parenting skills, but few skills of any other kind.

One solution to this type of problem might be to require the passage of a parenting test by any woman before she could become pregnant. In order to implement such a policy, it would be necessary to first develop a contraceptive that could be irreversibly inserted into the female body prior to puberty, and which would last over the rest of her reproductive-capable life unless an antidote were administered. If this entire idea seems ridiculous, think of how ridiculous it is that one of the most skill-demanding tasks in the world is undertaken routinely by millions of people who currently could never pass such a test.

Our Economy Is Population-based

Unfortunately, we have an economy that is dependent upon population expansion for its health. I say "unfortunately," because that brings with it all of the overpopulation-related problems, such as increased crime, deteriorating education, environmental pollution, and more rapid depletion of the earth's resources.

All one has to do in order to find support for this idea of a population-reliant economy is to examine any of the many commonly used economic-growth indicators, like housing starts, retail sales levels, and factory orders. All of those indicators are stimulated by the existence of an expanding population, and all of them would be stagnated by the stabilization of the population level. The primary economic indicator, the Gross Domestic Product, demonstrates this same dependence. The GDP is also, in many ways, an indicator of the rate of depletion of the earth's resources, in the form of the raw materials that go into the production of the manufactured products that are measured by it.

To examine just one of the above indicators, let's consider the number of housing starts. When the number of housing starts falls, gloom settles over the financial community. When the number of housing starts goes up, cheer reigns over moodsville. The bottomline about housing starts is that for the number to go up, it takes more people to want to build more homes.

There are, of course, many reasons why various individuals prefer an expansion of the population and oppose a reduction in the birth rate. Some have reasons that are based upon religion. Some, who don't have a religious reason, feel, nevertheless, that unlimited reproduction is an inalienable right, an attitude which may stem from the basic reproductive instincts that we all inherit through our genes. But, I suspect that there are some individuals who oppose a reduction in the birth rate primarily because of the impact that it would have on our economy. I would guess that the abundance of this type of individual would be in higher proportion among members of the business community than among the population in general, because the former rely for their personal economic health on the numbers of people who are consumers of their products and services.

For the sake of the health of our environment, I would like to see us switch to an economy that can maintain a healthy level in the face of the stabilization of the population level. One could hope for a conscious, intentional, worldwide conversion to an economy that is not dependent upon population expansion, because its inception would provide a positive environment for reduction in the birth rate. However, before the world's market powers will be willing to support the idea of a reduced birth rate, it is probably going to be necessary for some genius to design an economic plan that makes the health of the economy independent of population expansion.

123

The Solution To The Problem Of Pork-Barrel Politics

In the case of every so-called "pork-barrel" government project, it is possible to identify someone who considers that project to be "essential." If one were to examine all of the pork-barrel projects developed by congress, I'm confident that it would be discovered that the vast majority of those projects are designed primarily for the purpose of creating jobs. I say that because the most commonly voiced objections to the elimination of pork-barrel projects is that their demise would cost jobs. But, is it the government's responsibility to create jobs at the expense of enlarging the budget deficit?

I think that it's fairly safe to say that if all of the projects which were considered to be of the pork-barrel type by at least one member of congress were eliminated, the federal budget could be balanced quite easily. Why, then, aren't most pork-barrel projects eliminated from the federal budget? The answer is that the sponsors of every single pork-barrel project that ends up being included in the final budget have garnered enough votes for it to be approved. The average citizen doesn't understand very well how projects which are obviously of the pork-barrel type get passed in congress, but anyone who is thoroughly familiar with the wheeling-dealing and vote-swapping methodology of members of congress understands it *very* well.

So, the pork-barrel projects keep rolling along, and our national debt keeps getting larger and larger. Our worldwide credit standing and purchasing power decline significantly because our government is spending more money than it is taking in. Members of congress continue to label many of the projects sponsored by *other* members of congress as "pork-barrel," while at the same time they keep on seeking votes for their own self-indulging congressional bills.

Perhaps the answer is the establishment of a special Pork-barrel Division of congressional operations. Under newly established rules, a funding project could be assigned to the Pork-barrel Division of a chamber of congress if *ten per cent* of that chamber voted to have it defined as "pork-barrel." Once assigned to the Pork-barrel Division, that project would have to receive *eighty per cent* of the votes in that chamber in order to be approved for funding. A "pork-barrel" project could be defined as a project which benefits primarily those people who receive the project funds, either directly or indirectly. The relatively ambiguous term "primarily" would be included in order to permit the customary degree of congressional bickering.

The establishment of such a Pork-barrel Division might just be the answer to the problem of pork-barrel politics. Imagine the difficulty that a congressional sponsor would have in getting an eighty per cent approval of a bill that was labelled "pork-barrel" by at least ten per cent of the membership!

125

The Right-To-Life

The Right-To-Life Movement gets a lot of publicity about its opposition to abortion. Many of the more aggressive members of the movement can be seen in TV reports blockading medical clinics where abortions are performed. Some of the most aggressive members even initiate physical confrontations with people who are defending their rights to abortions. The word "murder" is used frequently by pro-life forces, who contend that human life begins at conception, rather than at birth as most pro-choice people contend. Although my emotional inclination is to favor the opinion of the pro-choice people on this, as a biologist I tend to agree with the definition of the beginning of life that is used by the pro-lifers.

Something that is unclear to me, however, is the right-to-life organization's stand on birth control that is effective in *preventing* conception: things like condoms and birth-control pills. I have yet to find in media reports any quotes that answer this nagging question. I suspect that most pro-life proponents oppose all artificial forms of birth control, and that they look upon the process of reproduction as an inalienable right that should be available to all humans to an uncontrolled extent. However, the right to reproduce ceases to be an inalienable one at the point at which the population level rises to where the birth rate creates more problems than the amount that can be solved. And, I personally believe that that point has

126

been reached. Some of the out-of-control problems that have been created by and exacerbated by over-population are crime, juvenile delinquency, decreased quality of education, inadequate health care, air pollution, water pollution, overexpansion of garbage dumps, depletion of plant resources such as timber, and depletion of animal resources such as salmon.

In debating the fate of the future of birth control, we may very well be deciding the fate of the human race. I consider it to be an undeniable fact that at the present rate of human population increase and consequent human destruction of the environment, we are headed inexorably toward the point at which the environment will be unfit for human life. It would be a relief to hear a prominent official of the Right-To-Life Movement proclaim that the movement supports the idea of birth control, as long as the birth control occurs before conception. That would be a major step in preventing the human population from self-destructing because of overpopulation. However, based on my observations of media coverage of the activities and proclamations of right-to-life officials thus far, I seriously doubt that such a proclamation will ever be made.

I strongly support many of the tenets of the right-to-life movement, but I personally don't believe that "right-to-life" includes "right-to-overpopulate."

Life's Goals

Have you ever wondered what was the purpose of the creation of your life here on earth, or what is the purpose of your existence? I think that it is very likely that the majority of the human population have never asked themselves such questions, but have, instead, merely followed their instincts in plodding through life, from beginning to end. Of the minority who have pondered those questions, it appears that a significant proportion have relied on their religious teachings to provide solace in that regard.

If, however, one ponders such questions, and does not find satisfaction in religious teachings, there is another approach that might be considered. It involves examining two very diverse sets of human characteristics. One is that set of characteristics that we have in common with all other living things. One phenomenon that we observe in this regard is that all living things possess a set of behaviors that are dedicated to promoting the survival of their respective species. Among plant life, those are generally referred to as "tropisms," and among animal life they are generally listed as "instincts."

Among the tropisms that are exhibited by plants are phototropism (response to light), geotropism (response to gravity), and hydrotropism (response to water). Scientists have concluded that these types of involuntary responses to the environment enhance the probability of the individual plant's survival, and thereby improve the chances of the plant species' perpetuation. Similarly, the *animal instincts* involved in activities such as feeding, reproduction, parenting, and escape from enemies all result in behaviors that improve the chances of the survival of the species. Humans, however, possess not only the kinds of *instincts* that are common among lower animals, but they also have advanced capabilities in the areas of logic and reasoning that effectively supplement those protective instincts.

At the other end of the spectrum, we might examine ways in which humans are di*fferent* from every other living species. One of those is that we have been provided with the ability to both feel and express emotions to a degree that is not found in any other form of life. And, in relation to that, we have a unique ability to recognize and feel *misery*, which is, of course, a potent factor in determining the *quality* of life. We undoubtedly have more awareness of our own quality of life, and are better able to assess it than is any other species.

Therefore, in response to the question that was advanced at the beginning of this discussion, let me say that if you have ever pondered your purpose for living, and if you are not satisfied with the answers which are provided by religious teachings, consider devoting your life in large degree to helping to preserve our species and helping to improve the quality of life among the members of our species. That approach could find justification in the fact that it addresses both something we *have in common with* all other forms of life, *and* a way in which we are *different from* all other forms of life.

Improving The Quality Of Life

If one accepts the idea that one of life's major purposes should be that of improving the quality of the human existence, one could begin a plan for pursuing such a goal by developing a list of the factors that affect quality of life. A factor that immediately comes to mind is that of the availability of adequate food. We are reminded of this almost daily by news reports about starvation. Another factor affecting the quality of human life is the relative degree of existence of freedom. Here, again, we are reminded of this almost daily by the hordes of foreigners who leave their native non-democratic countries and migrate to democracies, particularly the United States. Although many of those migrants come here because of the *economic* opportunities, those opportunities are an undeniable result of the *political* freedoms which we enjoy.

Another factor that affects our quality of life is the level of our knowledge and skills, which are dependent largely upon the quality of our education. Still another related factor is the overall quality of our environment, and there are, of course, numerous ways in which that can be reduced to a point which creates physical or emotional stress for us.

Another quality-reduction factor is the whole set of medical problems, which can occur as a result of disease, accidents, or aging. And still another is the interaction between our environment (both living and non-living components) and our emotional makeup.

Many people who have no unsatisfied physical needs in life are, nevertheless, traumatized because of elements that create emotional stress.

If you have a desire to help to improve the quality of life of human beings, you might begin by examining a list such as the foregoing one, and by identifying from it some factors which you could confront in one or more ways, large or small, to reduce human misery. One approach would be to contribute time, energy, or money to one of the existing charitable organizations. Another might be to provide relief directly to one or more individuals. That might consist of a variety of activities, including, but not limited to help with daily chores, educational instruction, or entertainment. A useful method of solving *many* stress-producing problems is to become involved in politics in a manner, either direct or indirect, that helps to produce quality-enhancing legislation.

Finally, because so many sources of human misery are related to *overpopulation*, one might take a broad approach, and work to improve the overall, total quality of life of the human race by reducing the human population in humane ways. That could include volunteer work for organizations like Planned Parenthood or Zero Population Growth, or contributions to those and similar organizations.

Species Preservation

If we accept the idea that one of life's major goals should be the preservation and perpetuation of the human species, we might plan the pursuit of that goal by examining the major current threats to the existence of our species. A list that is not all-inclusive might contain subjects such as the collision of the earth with an asteroid, disease epidemics, global warming, a reduction in the ozone layer, all forms of pollution, lack of food, and nuclear war. I find it interesting to note that all except one of those factors are related to human population levels. That one exception is the asteroid problem, which has been advanced as a scientifically supported reason for the fairly rapid extinction of the dinosaurs. A prominent hypothesis that is currently under consideration by the scientific community is that the earth was struck by an asteroid several millions ago, and that the impact almost instantaneously killed most forms of existing life, including the dinosaurs. Although the asteroid problem might seem to be beyond human control, there are some scientists who are working on the development of techniques for diverting asteroids from potentially deadly courses by using nuclear explosions.

Each of the other threats that is listed above can be shown to be related in some way, either directly or indirectly, to human population levels. The population-level connection of the threat of disease epidemic might initially escape one, but it is related because of the fact that the ease with which most diseases spread depends to a large extent upon the population density within the geographical area in which the disease organism exists.

The connection between all of the other listed threats and population levels should be more obvious, although one might wonder about nuclear war. The link is that wars are more likely to occur between groups of people who have conflicting interests, and the likelihood of such conflicts is greater among groups that are forced, through population pressures, to have excessive interaction with each other.

The fact that most of the listed factors are related to human population levels might cause one to speculate that a way to reduce the threat of all of them might be to reduce the human population level. If that were established as a goal, it should be achieved, naturally, only by using humane methods such as condoms and birth-control pills.

There are, of course, many people who strongly resist the idea of population control. Some of them have reasons that are based upon religion. Others have economic reasons. And still others have reasons that stem from the pressures of our basic reproductive instincts. But, we are talking here about *survival of the human species.* And in such a context, all of the reasons for opposing population controls might pale by comparison to the dire alternative which faces us.

Species Survival

One of the characteristics that is common to most of the species of higher non-plant life is the possession of a set of instincts. Most of those instincts act to help prevent the overall species from becoming extinct. Probably the most powerful of all of the instincts are the ones associated with successful reproduction, without which any species would rapidly disappear. One example of a manifestation of a reproductive instinct is that of the male salmon fiercely driving off any rival which approaches his mate and her nest. Another is that of the male duck which aggressively repels any other male that demonstrates designs toward the female duck that he has selected as his own. Actions of these types probably help to assure procreation of the fittest of the species.

Undoubtedly the most powerful of the reproductive instincts is the sex drive, which very well may reach its peak among the human species, wherein it is intertwined with conscious thought processes. Clever advertisers take advantage of this fact, as one can witness by viewing the emphasis on sex appeal that is present in TV commercials about beer, clothing, automobiles, and many other products, including some as mundane as margarine and crackers.

The fact that the reproductive instincts which are possessed by animals like fish and birds are also present in the human species can be witnessed by any person who observes a typical crowd in a shopping mall on an average day. However, a major difference between us and animals like fish and birds is that we have been blessed with the ability to use logic and reasoning in order to both supplement and counteract our basic instincts. And that may be the major characteristic that sets us apart from all other forms of life.

The human race is rapidly approaching a point at which it is imperative that logic and reasoning be employed to counteract our reproductive instincts. Of all of the species living today, the human species is the only one that possesses the ability to damage its own environment to the point of species extinction. Such extinction might result from the radioactivity of nuclear explosions, from cancer caused by reduction of the ozone layer, from deadly levels of air pollution, from lethal levels of water pollution, or from one of many other factors that are related either directly or indirectly to human population density. The excess of human population threatens to damage our environment to a point that it becomes intolerable for human life. Our logic and reasoning abilities should tell us that it would be very prudent of us to apply the birth control technology which we have developed (through logic and reasoning), in order to reduce the human population to a level at which the threat of extinction of our species is eliminated.

We Need More Thinking Skills Instruction

One of the characteristics that sets apart the human species from all other living species is the possession of advanced capabilities for applying logic and reasoning. Some people prefer to refer to those applications as "thinking skills." And, whereas other forms of life have to rely on physically oriented tropisms or instincts as their major pathways to assuring the perpetuation of their species, humans have the potential for these unusual me*ntal* abilities to help in that process. However, our having the *potential* doesn't mean that every human individual develops those skills to the maximum possible extent.

After a thorough examination of numerous instructional programs in the area of thinking skills, I have arrived at the following succinct and composite definition: "Thinking skills are those skills which are involved in the analysis of information and the formation of ideas based upon that analysis." It has been demonstrated that formal instruction in thinking skills can not only hasten development of those skills, but can also increase the *total* degree to which they are developed. That being the case, it is disheartening to note that, in our schools, very little emphasis is placed upon instruction in the thinking skills.

Unfortunately, the overwhelming bulk of educational instruction is devoted to the *acquisition* of information, while very little emphasis is given to the *analysis* of information, with consequent development of ideas. The paucity of thinking-skills instruction is not due to a complete lack of thinking-skills goals among school districts, however. I have examined the lists of broad goals of many school districts, and have found almost all of those lists to include a goal pertaining to the need for instruction in thinking skills. However, when one examines what is actually happening in the classrooms of those school districts, it can be found that very little instruction in thinking skills is occurring. One exception to that general observation is that of gifted-child programs, which are often accomplished through arrangements involving separate school buildings or classrooms for gifted students, and which are devoted to distinctive instruction for those "special" students.

The scarcity of thinking-skills instruction is revealed in many ways. One is the absence of those skills as a curricular subject on report cards. Another is the failure of schools to designate specific amounts or blocks of time for such instruction. A third is the lack of routine testing of overall student populations for their level of such skills. Actually, if any school district accomplished all three of those, I would consider it to be serious about teaching thinking skills, but without *any* of the three, dedication to improving thinking skills would appear to be lacking.

Being Successful In Business

I once asked a very successful entrepreneur if he had any advice for me as I was searching for a business venture. His reply was, "Find a niche, and fill it." After thinking for a while about his statement, I translated it as follows: "Identify an unmet human need, and then develop a product or service to meet that need." Perhaps one of the primary characteristics that distinguishes successful inventors and entrepreneurs from the rest of us is their ability to recognize needs that are *unmet*. That is probably just as important to their accomplishments as is their ability to *develop* the product or service which satisfies the need.

In order to identify *products* that have been created in answer to human needs, one has only to survey the vast array of items that are available in the typical hardware store. Some common examples include the electronic barbecue fire starter, the can of temporary puncture-seal for tubeless tires, and the rechargeable battery-operated screw-driver.

In order to identify a long list of *services* which have come about as a result of unmet human needs, one need only look through the Yellow Pages directory. There you find references to numerous highly specialized services, from automation systems, bridal gown preservation, and colonic irrigation, to x-ray silver recovery service, yoga therapy, and zipper repair.

One of the main keys to identifying unmet human

needs is the ability to *realize* that they are *really* needs, and that they are *really* unmet. A method of accomplishing this is to think in terms of what people would like to be able to do that they can't do, or what they would like to have that they don't have. The fact that there are innumerable unmet human needs is manifested by the expression of often-voiced complaints from acquaintances about tasks they wish they could accomplish but don't know how to accomplish.

One way to initiate the process of perceiving unmet human needs is to think about a variety of daily human activities and all of the existing impediments to ideal performance of those activities. In the case of almost any human endeavor that one can identify, it is possible to recognize a stress-producing factor, the elimination of which could make that task much easier. One of the skills that could help to make a person a prosperous entrepreneur is that of envisioning a wide variety of hypothetical human activities, and the range of theoretical barriers to their ideal accomplishment.

If you are a person who is tired of working for someone else and who would like to start your own business, perhaps you should consider developing the skill of identifying unmet human needs. You might find that once you have done that, the processes of developing products and services to meet such needs are easier to acquire than you have previously thought them to be.

X-Genes And Y-Genes

Most women inherit *two* X-chromosomes, and most men inherit *one* X-chromosome which is paired with a Y-chromosome. On the X-chromosome there are some genes, which I will call X-genes. They are recessive, which means that they only manifest themselves if a person has two of them. On the Y-chromosome, there are some genes which I will call Y-genes. They are dominant, which means that they manifest themselves even if the person has only one of them.

One X-gene is the "shopping gene." That gene causes one to be interested in shopping for hours on end, even when one has no money to spend. The effects of the shopping gene are exacerbated by the availability of easy credit, which permits one to ignore the fact that purchased items eventually have to be paid for. An important manifestation of the shopping gene is that it causes one to go shopping without any particular purchase in mind; instead, it causes one to *look for things to spend money on*, even if they aren't needed by the shopper.

Another X-gene is the "talking gene," which enables one to talk for hours on end about unimportant topics. The talking gene expresses itself to the ultimate level when three or more people who possess that gene get together. Under these circumstances, thoughts are primarily coming out of the brain of the "talking gene" possessor, but hardly any thoughts are going into that person's brain. Another way of saying this is that the possessor of the "talking gene" is doing a lot of talking but very little listening.

You might have already inferred that *Y-genes* are possessed primarily by *males*. One of the Y-genes is the "beat 'em" gene, which causes possessors of that gene to want to beat other possessors of that gene at anything and everything, from fights-to-the-death to watermelon-seed-spitting. The most common manifestation of the "beat 'em" gene is the sports nut who is glued to the TV set while the world falls apart around him. It is probably the "beat 'em" gene that is responsible for the fact that the average life span of men is so much shorter than that of women.

Another Y-gene is the "play gene." This gene makes play highly desired by the possessor, and any kind of work tremendously loathsome. One of the human activities that is most antagonistic to the "play gene" is housework. Some activities which are generally soothing to the "play gene" are hunting, fishing, bowling, beer-drinking in taverns, and impromptu sandlot football games.

I have mentioned here just a few of the X-genes and Y-genes. You probably realize that there are many more such genes, all of which make life both interesting and frustrating.

Our Kids Shouldn't Have It Any Better Than We Did

I frequently hear a parent say, "I want my kids to have it better than I did." And that often comes from people who didn't really suffer much deprivation, if any, during their childhood. Perhaps they didn't have everything they *wanted*, but they may very well have had everything they *needed*. I get the feeling that when people say such things, they feel that their children should have less stress and austerity in their lives, and more material things.

According to my observations, most "kids" seem to feel that they are entitled to at least as good a life style during their young adult years as their parents currently have. A lot of today's parents of young adults have a comfortable home, at least one trouble-free car for transportation, relatively nutritious and delicious meals, and many other components of what we usually consider to be a part of the "American Dream." What many of the young adults don't realize is that their parents didn't start out married life with all of those amenities. Many of those parents may have lived in rented one-bedroom apartments, may have had to take the bus much of the time, and may have had a diet that consisted largely of macaroni and cheese during their early years of marriage.

One phenomenon that has occurred on a regular basis is that wise and frugal young married couples gradually accumulate wealth and improve their standard of living. By the time that many of them have children who are of adolescent age or older, they have enough wealth to support a relatively comfortable standard of living for the entire family. Many of the young adults who emerge from that stage of their parents' lives want to get married and start married life at their parents *current* level of standard of living rather than at their *initial* standard of living. In many cases of this type, one of the few ways that the newlyweds can maintain such a life style is to live on a relatively high degree of credit, which reduces significantly the probability that they will ever accumulate much real wealth. Another possibility is to turn to illegal activities to support their artificially high standard of living.

Actually, deprivation during one's childhood can be a great character builder. It can make us aware of the fact that many people in the world suffer that kind of deprivation throughout their entire lives. It can also make us appreciative of having all of the *necessities*, and help us to put less emphasis on the fact that we might not have all of the *luxuries* that we want. With that in mind, it might be a good policy for parents to artificially create deprivation in the lives of their children occasionally, even if their financial situations could enable them to avoid such conditions. Children who have never been exposed to any kind of stressful living conditions can enter adulthood with a very unrealistic view of the way that the world works.

Let's Eliminate Governmental 'Drip-bucket' Projects

In the old days, when the roof would leak, we would place a bucket under the dripping water, and that was how the leak in the roof was solved. Of course, the problem of the leak wasn't *really* solved; only the drip, the symptom of the leak, was dealt with. Today, it can be observed that governments at all levels - city, county, state, and federal - undertake "drip-bucket" programs to deal with symptoms rather than the basic problems which underlie those symptoms. One particularly notable example is the needle exchange program for drug addicts. The alleged goal is to keep addicts from contracting AIDS. What we're doing in reality is preserving the lives of those addicts and thus putting them in a position to spread their debilitating habit to others.

Another noteworthy drip-bucket policy which is found mainly at the federal level is that of bailing out troubled insured funds, such as the Federal Savings And Loan Insurance Corporation, and the HUD program of insured loans. As we are now beginning to realize, government-insured funds attract numerous unscrupulous entrepreneurs who view the existence of those funds as an opportunity to justify high-risk investments. By bailing out those funds and their investors, we are encouraging the continuation of the practices that got them into trouble in the first place.

144

A type of drip-bucket program that arouses extreme emotions, and which would undoubtedly stir up heated debate if opposed, are some of the feeding programs, which are aimed at feeding the starving people in foreign lands. In examining the populations of many of those lands, we find that many of them are experiencing uncontrolled birth rates, which simply exacerbate the starvation problem. By providing free food, we are promoting the survival of people who go on to give birth to more babies, who in turn need more food, and who thus contribute to the seriousness of the situation.

Probably the most gigantic of all problems that are being approached in drip-bucket fashion is the overpopulation problem. Overpopulation can result in reduced quality of education, increased crime, increased government intrusion into private lives, increased taxes, environmental damage, and a whole host of other symptoms. Governments all over the world expend major portions of their resources on programs to deal with these symptoms, and they, according to my way of thinking, have to come under the heading of drip-bucket programs. Rarely, if ever, does a government take steps to reduce the basic, underlying problem, which is overpopulation.

It seems clear to me that if we seriously attempted to avoid drip-bucket programs and sought, instead, to eliminate the basic problems which underlie the symptoms at which the drip-bucket programs are aimed, our resources would go a lot further toward making the world a better place to live in.

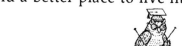

Selecting The Survivors
Of Our Species

Suppose that the environment became so badly
damaged that it was no longer fit for human
life. And suppose that we knew a few years before-
hand that such a situation was going to develop. And
suppose further, that we were able to build an artificial environment in an enclosed structure, which I
will call an "envirodome." And, finally, suppose that
we had time to select thirty people to remain as the
last survivors of the human race by being sealed in the
envirodome, safe from the hostile outside environment.

If all the above suppositions ever came to pass,
what would be the criteria for selecting the thirty
people to carry on our kind? Wouldn't we want them
to be outstanding representatives of our species? But,
then, "outstanding" in respect to what characteristics? A few that quickly come to mind are intelligence,
knowledge, and physical health.

How would we select them for intelligence? Would
we use I.Q. test results? Or would we simply reflect
upon their manifestations of superior intelligence,
such as outstanding accomplishments in intellectual
fields?

How would we assess their knowledge? Would
we give priority to knowledge in specific fields of
study, or to overall general knowledge of everyday
types of topics? Physical health might be relatively

easy to evaluate, by using the results of performance on various kinds of exercise equipment.

In addition to the three foregoing types of characteristics for use in selecting the survivors of the human race, there is the group of characteristics that is specific to each race within the human species. Wouldn't we want to send as diverse as possible a group into the haven that would house the procreators of our descendants for all time? If the answer is "Yes," then which races should comprise the group of thirty? And, don't forget that we're undoubtedly talking about both a male and female of each of those races, and verifiedly fertile individuals, to be sure. That would limit the sample to fifteen races. The task of selecting the chosen fifteen could be awesome.

What about the genetics of the thirty selectees? Wouldn't we want to make sure that they were genetically pure representatives of their alleged race? And then what about checking for absence of defective genes, by DNA analysis? Wouldn't we want to make sure that our descendants were free of such genes? But, then, what is a "defective" gene? Arriving at a definition that was acceptable to all who had voting power on this issue would be an overwhelming responsibility.

If this entire discussion seems irrelevant to you, please reflect on the fact that the damage to the environment by the human population is accumulating at an ever-increasing rate, and it might not be very many years before we are faced with choices such as those theorized above.

Should We Build An Envirodome?

The idea that the environment might become
unfit for human life is not completely far-
fetched, considering the multitude of ways in which
it is currently being damaged or in danger of being
damaged. There are the problems of pollution, both
atmospheric and aquatic. Then there are the hazards
of nuclear war or nuclear accidents: radioactivity or
nuclear winter. There are also global warming, the
destruction of the ozone layer, a theoretically destruc-
tive imbalance in the oxygen-carbon dioxide ratio of
the atmosphere, and the possibility of a collision between the earth and an asteroid. Those are just a few
of the factors threatening the tolerability of the environment.

Well, suppose that the environment in which we
humans live *did* become unfit for human life. What
plans could we make ahead of time that would help
at least a few of us to survive and perpetuate our
species? One possibility is the construction of an enclosure in which an artificial, benign environment
could be maintained. I will refer, henceforth, to such
an enclosure by the name "envirodome." In order to
support human life on a long-term basis, it would
have to provide the basic necessities that are required
in order for our life processes to be carried out. Some
of the fundamental ones would be feeding, breathing,
and waste disposal. There are many others that could
be mentioned, but those three alone would present

significant challenges to our ingenuity. They have been the focus of experimentation in a project called the "Biosphere," which has involved an enclosure that was totally sealed off from the outside environment, and in which attempts were made to maintain a balanced ecosystem that could support humans completely independently of the outside.

Although I have never heard it said that the purpose of the Biosphere project was to prepare for environmental Armageddon, that project might certainly have taught us things that will be helpful if such a catastrophe ever actually occurs. However, one great flaw in the Biosphere project is that it assumes that sunlight would be available to drive the ecosystem. But, at least two of the threats to the stability of our environment could result in the shutting-out of light from the surface of the earth. Those two are nuclear winter and collision with an asteroid. One possible solution to the problem of a lack of light might be the utilization of an efficient source of energy such as fusion. If fusion energy were available in an envirodome, it could be transformed into light energy, which could then be used to perpetuate the ecosystem inside.

Just on the outside chance that the environment might be damaged to the point of intolerability for human life, perhaps we should be developing a practical method of harnessing fusion, and maybe we should be building at least one envirodome, into which we côuld hurriedly herd the last few surviving humans.

149

A Permanent I.D. Number
For Every Newborn

M uch outrage has been voiced over so-called "government intrusion" into citizens' private lives. New computerized methods of record-keeping by banks, telephone companies, transportation companies, and utility companies, among others, have not only improved the operations of those groups, but have also facilitated useful record-*checking* by them and law enforcement agencies.

One factor that effectively facilitates the computerized search of records is the existence of the Social Security Number. Unfortunately, many people either use a false number or don't have one. Perhaps the solution to this flaw in the record-keeping system is to assign a permanent identification number to every newborn baby and to every immigrant entering this country permanently. That number could be attached indelibly to a part of the person's body, such as a tattoo on the inside of the wrist. Or, using some of the emerging technology, perhaps a tiny encoded capsule could be implanted irreversibly beneath the skin. There is even the possibility that, with the improvements that are being made in DNA analysis, that technique could be used as a determiner of one's identification.

If one of the foregoing methods of permanently attaching an I.D. number to one's body were used, it could greatly simplify many of the procedures in our daily lives. For example, one would no longer have to carry a wallet full of identification cards for all of the organizations to which they belonged. We wouldn't have to get out our wallet and find the right card every time we had to identify ourselves and confirm our membership or eligibility. Stores selling alcoholic beverages would find it very easy to confirm one's age. Police would be able to check suspects' identification quite simply.

The requirement of a permanent readable I.D. number that could be easily determined by aiming a piece of equipment at any member of the population could be coupled with the creation of a permanent cumulative record on every individual, that record to be established in and retrievable from the national computer system. Not only would that combination facilitate the work of law enforcement agencies, but it could make life easier for the individual by eliminating tasks such as the need to fill out an identification form and complete family history every time one wanted to apply for a job or enter a medical facility. Prospective employers, doctors, and hospitals could simply call up your cumulative record on their computers.

Although the suggested identification and record system could make our lives much easier, I suspect that the average citizen would not be willing to give up their current status of relative anonymity in order to receive those benefits. After all, anonymity gives us a high degree of protection from having to accept responsibility for our actions.

Immigration

I'm beginning to think that immigration into the United States should be stopped. I didn't used to feel that way; I was highly influenced by the argument that our nation was originally built by immigrants and that it continued to thrive for many decades, through the constructive efforts of immigrants. During that period, there arose occasional objections to allowing immigration, especially objections based on the development of problems due to overpopulation and competition for jobs. However, almost without exception, we developed new technologies which at least temporarily overcame those types of objections.

Now I am beginning to change my mind. In recent years we have seen a flood of *illegal* immigrants into this country, and that exacerbates any problems that could result from *legal* immigration. That wave of immigrants causes me to reflect on the fact that immigration in the early years of our country occurred during times when both our natural resources and our environment seemed to be unlimited. We are now finding that our natural resources are *not* limitless. Also, we are becoming increasingly aware of the limitations on the ability of the environment to accommodate an ever-increasing population.

In addition, most of the earlier immigration was legal, and legal immigrants were required to learn English in order to obtain citizenship. Although the practice of requiring all citizens to learn the same language is labeled "racist" by many people today, it did have the advantage of enhancing communication between all citizens, and one of the best ways to reduce conflicts among people is to increase communication between them.

A third problem which may be even less obvious than the first two is that up until now, this country has been living on credit. For the first few decades it was in the form of drawing upon the symbolic "money in the bank" represented by our abundant natural resources. During the twentieth century, living on credit reared its head in the form of extensive deficit spending. The relationship between credit spending and the advantages or disadvantages of immigration is that such spending by any entity, whether it be an individual or a national government, allows that entity to artificially and temporarily improve its standard of living. One of the aspects of that artificial improvement is the creation of jobs. So, for most of the history of our country, we were able, by credit spending, to create jobs for most of the people who needed them. Now we're at a point where deficit spending itself is on the verge of wreaking economic havoc, so that it can no longer be safely expanded. Well, if we are no longer in a position to artificially create jobs for an expanding population, perhaps we should be thinking about ways to reduce that expansion. One of them could be to reduce or eliminate immigration.

Investment Risk

I have never invested money in any venture that involved any more risk than that of a federally insured bank account. I still recommend strongly to people that they not invest in anything riskier than that, unless they could afford to lose the investment without suffering any serious deprivation in terms of the necessities of life. My recommendation stems from my belief that any investments which I make should be primarily for the purpose of *preserving* my purchasing power, as opposed to *increasing* my purchasing power. According to my way of thinking, everyone except those who make their basic living through investing should rely primarily on their *main job* to *increase* their net worth, and should rely on investments only to *protect* their net worth.

This attitude of mine flies in the face of the conventional wisdom that is expressed by most of my acquaintances. Most of *them* have investments that involve significantly higher risks than those which are characteristic of insured bank accounts. Their investments include high yield ventures such as mutual funds, individual stocks, venture capital investments, and highly mortgaged real estate. All of those, of course, have the mutual characteristic of being somewhat dependent for their yields upon an expanding population and a healthy, expanding economy. I notice that most of those acquaintances read the financial pages of the newspaper daily, and eye nervously any indications that the health of the economy might be declining. Also, many of them frequently switch their money from one kind of investment to another in order to take advantage of rapidly changing economic trends. I suppose that kind of activity is acceptable as long as one enjoys it, but it appears to me that many of my acquaintances experience quite a lot of stress in the process, always worrying that "the bottom will fall out" of this or that financial market, leaving them with worthless investments. Personally, I experience a lot of comfort in knowing that my money is invested in a low-risk manner, so that I don't have to worry continuously about the status of local, state, national, and world economies.

Many financial advisors who have discovered that I am relatively secure, financially speaking (even though not rich), have approached me with proposals for putting money into their various high-yield investments. It has always turned out, of course, that those high-yield investments were also high-*risk* investments. Financial advisors have bombarded me over and over again with the statement, "You should have your money *working* for you." Actually, I suspect that what they really want is *my* money working for *them.*

We Need A Process-centered Curriculum

In the year 1967, a revolutionary elementary school science program was published. It had been developed under the auspices of the American Association for the Advancement of Science, and was dubbed the Triple-A, S Program. The reason why I refer to it as "revolutionary" is that it had a basic structure that was different from that of the other existing elementary science programs. The latter emphasized, almost without exception, the accumulation of knowledge, and were structured around a list of scientific subject areas, such as Air, Heat, Light, Water, etc. The AAAS program, on the other hand, emphasized primarily the development of what it termed "the scientific processes." Those included the following: Observing, Using Space/Time Relationships, Using Numbers, Measuring, Classifying, Communicating, Predicting, Inferring, Formulating Hypotheses, Controlling Variables, Interpreting Data, Defining Operationally, and Experimenting. The learning of scientific information was not excluded from the AAAS program, but was, however, to be learned incidentally to the development of the processes.

It didn't take me long to realize that what the AAAS called the "scientific processes" could just as easily be termed "intellectual processes," and that they could just as well be taught in conjunction with some of the other subjects of the curriculum. They also seemed to overlap extensively with skills and processes which we commonly give names like "logic," "reasoning," "thinking skills," and "common sense." I realized that skill with the AAAS processes was woefully lacking in our populace and that virtually no formal instruction in those processes occurred in our schools. Consequently, I approached the curriculum director of our school district with the proposal that we develop a new curricular framework consisting of the "intellectual processes" that were defined by the AAAS program, and that we expect the specialists in each subject matter area to teach those processes in conjunction with their respective factual matter. My proposal got nowhere.

Well, the AAAS program never did get off the ground nationwide, for a variety of reasons. Among them were the inertia of the existing memorization-based science programs and the lack of teaching staff who were trained to teach according to the new process-based methodology. So, we still have primarily memorization-based, fact-centered curricular programs in the United States, and there is still a woeful lack of skill in the use of the intellectual processes. Perhaps it's time that we considered the adoption of a process-centered curriculum.

Problem-Solving Skills

The possession of abundant knowledge does not, in and of itself, make a person a good problem solver. Many parents erroneously believe that they can train their children to become good problem solvers by simply exposing them to experiences that increase their knowledge. During my 32 years in the field of education, I observed numerous students who had abundant knowledge, yet who were not good problem solvers. On the other hand, I observed many students who had poor memories, and thus limited knowledge, but who were relatively skilled at problem-solving.

The accumulation of knowledge requires primarily the process of remembering. Two more advanced levels of processing information are *understanding* it, and being able to *apply* it to new situations. I had many students who could remember a specific bit of information, but who really didn't understand it, and who manifested that shortcoming by not being able to apply the information. In addition, I encountered some students who remembered information and understood it, but who were nevertheless unable to apply it. In most instances, students who are able to apply information are able to remember it and understand it, but the converse is not true.

Students who can remember and understand information, and then apply it don't necessarily have good problem-solving skills, however, because the process of problem-solving involves even more advanced levels of mental operations. In order to be a good problem solver, one must be able to analyze all sorts of information, and to then synthesize from that information a solution or a new idea that is based upon their analysis. To put it another way, in order to be a good problem solver, a person must be able to examine all of the information related to a problem, and to be able to distinguish similarities, differences, and ambiguities among the various items of information. They must then be able to utilize that analysis as the basis for formulating a solution to the problem. People who lack the ability to analyze information and to synthesize new ideas from it are usually not good problem solvers.

When I first started noticing details of the problem-solving skills of students, I found it to be relatively easy to understand why those who had abundant knowledge without having analytical and synthesizing abilities were not good problem solvers, but I found it difficult to understand why students who had poor memories for information could sometimes be above average problem solvers. An understanding of the latter situation came easily once I realized that poor memory does not necessarily preclude the ability to analyze and synthesize well.

Why Ask Questions?

Have you ever been in a meeting involving a large group, and wanted to ask the speaker a question, but felt so intimidated by the presence of the others in attendance that you avoided asking it? It appears to me that the *majority* of people in whose minds questions arise are too timid to ask their questions in front of a group. Actually, there is no better way to clear up uncertainty about what a speaker has said than to ask them a direct question about it. I discovered that concept many years ago.

Both the reluctance of people to ask questions in large groups, and the benefits of asking questions can be illustrated by describing two incidents that occurred during my college years. The first involved a graduate-level class that I was taking. After only a few days in the course, I found that the instructor frequently made statements, the point of which I couldn't understand. So, as was my custom, I began asking questions about any ambiguous statements. Well, he rapidly became irritated by my frequent questioning, and I tried my best to avoid feeling inferior because I was the only one in the class who asked any questions, and perhaps the only one who didn't understand the instructor. After several weeks in the course, I got the flu and missed two days of class. When I returned to class after my illness, a student in the seat next to me leaned over and whispered to me, "We're sure glad you're back. We haven't understood a thing he's said while you've been gone!"

The second incident involved a summer institute that was funded by the National Science Foundation. Supposedly, the students who were recruited to attend that institute were the forty best high school and community college biology teachers from the northwestern United States. The weekly schedule of the institute involved lab work and lectures Monday through Thursday. On Friday afternoon we usually had a test over the foregoing four days of studies. Well, on this one particular Friday afternoon, we all sat down at our desks, and the instructor handed out the week's test. As I perused the questions on the test, I quickly got the feeling that I wasn't familiar with the material that they covered. But, I looked around and everyone else was writing answers furiously. So I took my test up to the instructor. He took one look at my test and said, "This is *next week's test.* Your class hasn't covered this material yet!" Thinking that I was the only student who had received the wrong test, I asked him for a copy of the appropriate one. It was then that he discovered that he had handed-out the wrong test to *everyone.* In other words, we weren't yet *supposed* to be familiar with the concepts covered on that test. It was interesting to note that everyone but me assumed that they should know the answers, and they were writing what turned out to be completely inappropriate answers in their test booklets.

I hope that the foregoing stories illustrate convincingly the advisability of asking questions when you don't understand something.

Governmental Restrictions

R ecently I have heard a lot of complaints about
various types of governmental restrictions.
Most of them have been about limitations caused by
zoning laws and environmental regulations. Ostensi-
bly, the purpose of such laws and regulations is to
attempt to preserve the quality of life which we have
come to expect as part of the "American Dream." That
includes things like clean air, unpolluted water, abundant recreational spaces, uncrowded living conditions, litter-free neighborhoods, and uncongested roads.
It should surprise no one that as the population density of any geographical area increases, all of the
aforementioned aspects of the American Dream become threatened.

It is inevitable that as population increases in an
area, restrictions on human activities in that area are
going to have to be established in order to protect
people from each other. The average citizen who com-
plains about zoning laws apparently doesn't realize
that almost all of those laws have been written in
order to protect the majority of the residents in the
affected areas from having their standard of living or
life style eroded. One type of zoning law that I have
observed to be protested by many citizens is the type
that prevents someone from parking a recreational
vehicle in their driveway for extended periods. If one
lives in the country, where there is only one house
every mile or so along the roadway, there is no need

for that type of law because the overall quality of the environment is not reduced significantly by the presence of an occasional parked recreational vehicle. However, in an area of high population density, where there may be a house on every lot, the abundance of parked recreational vehicles may get to such a level that that is the main thing that the passer-by sees.

Another type of law that is resented by a lot of citizens is the type that requires permits for various types of construction in residential areas. Well, again, if you live out in the sparsely inhabited countryside, any kind of construction that you perform on your home or adjacent land is not going to have much of an impact on other people. But, if you live in a highly populated area, such construction can have a relatively large impact on your neighbors. For example, your construction might crowd them excessively, or it might block part of their view.

Paradoxically, land developers, who complain vociferously about zoning laws and environmental restrictions, stand to gain the most from rapid population growth, which, of course, eventually results in the environmental concerns that *lead* to the establishment of those laws and restrictions. It is amazing to me that most people seem oblivious to the relationship between population density and the need for governmental restrictions.

Are Humans Born Selfish?

I have been told by many altruistic people that they think that humans are born unselfish, but that many *learn* to be *selfish* as they grow older. Personally, I think that the reverse is true. I think that humans are born basically *selfish,* and that they learn to be unselfish through proper guidance. All of the evidence that I need to support my position on this can be obtained by observing just about any infants, toddlers, pre-pubescents, or adolescents. The earliest sound that we hear from most newborns is the wailing that signals that they have some need that they want satisfied. It may be a need for food, diaper changing, or some other need, but their cries continue until heeded. Where is the display of unselfishness among these wails? This total emphasis on satisfaction of self-needs continues through infancy, and most parents slavishly cater to their offsprings' blatant demands.

At the toddler stage, the self-indulging instinct is prominently displayed through attitude toward toys. Anyone who has spent much time around a group of toddlers can't help but have heard shrieks of "Mine" or "My toy" when some other child picks up the shrieker's toy. It is very common to observe the parents of the screaming child reminding him or her that we share our toys, and that we don't need more than one toy at a time. Through patient, continued guidance of this type, it is possible to instill the philosophy of sharing in the growing child.

By the time children reach the pre-pubescent stage, it can be observed that careful direction by parents has caused the majority to adopt basically unselfish attitudes. However, at the adolescent stage, when the sex hormones begin to flow, selfishness once again rears its ugly head. The influence of the sex hormones creates a new need that must be satisfied, and causes a new era of self-centeredness. That era lasts until the attitude of unselfishness makes a major comeback in adult individuals when they become parents. At that point, the cycle starts all over again. The newborn offspring manifest their unmet needs by loud wails, and the new parents are instinctively led to expend their financial, physical, and emotional resources on the new arrivals.

Vestiges of the selfish attitude with which we are born linger throughout the adult life of a few people. One is cutting in line at the ticket booth. Another is racing the other drivers for the last parking space near the entrance to the supermarket. We see these behaviors almost everywhere we go. However, thanks to proper upbringing, the basic selfishness with which we are born has been overcome in *most* humans by the time that they reach maturity. But in a few adults, the toddler's cries of "My toy, mine!" are replaced by hostile thoughts of "My parking space, mine!"

The Maximum Sentence Shouldn't Exceed 5 Years

Have you ever considered how much it costs to house the criminals who are in our prisons? Thousands of dollars are spent each year to provide room and board for each convicted felon. In the case of many of them, that cost continues for many years. All the while, they are enjoying a standard of living that is much higher than what the majority of the rest of the world's population has. One of the easiest pathways to a guaranteed minimum standard of living is to receive a prison sentence in the United States. We're spending at least as much to house convicted felons as we spend on support and education of the law-abiding poor. Well, maybe the situation should be reversed. Perhaps we should spend more on helping those poor people, and less on assuring prisoners of not only three meals a day, but also many amenities that the poverty-stricken can only dream about.

One way to reduce prison costs would be to cut down on the prisoner population, but not by reducing law enforcement or prosecution of criminals or the sentences of the convicts. Perhaps we should adopt a policy of sentencing convicted felons to no more than five years of prison time. That suggestion may come as a shock to you, but wait, there is more! The suggested policy would include a stipulation that if a panel of social workers and psychologists were to conclude that the convicted criminal was incapable of being completely rehabilitated within the maximum five-year sentencing period, that convict would be executed. In order to reduce recidivism, there should probably also be added the following condition: the mandatory execution of released felons who later committed another felony. Now that, my friends, should give those who are contemplating the commission of a crime something to think about! It should also give convicted felons a lot of motivation to prove to the authorities that they can be rehabilitated. Imagine the significant increase in rehabilitation rate that would result from the adoption of this policy!

This suggestion is destined to be condemned by those who routinely defend the rights of prisoners to not be subjected to "cruel and unusual punishment," and who often seem more protective of convicts' civil rights than those of the rest of the population. The punishment that is suggested here may seem very harsh, but it would cause less suffering than that imposed by ordinary daily life upon the majority of honest poverty stricken people. Those people could benefit tremendously if the money that was saved by this new practice was shifted toward improving their welfare. And, if those funds were available to pay for food, housing, education, and all of the other basic components of a decent minimal standard of living for the non-criminal segment of the population, there would probably be much less crime committed.

Let's Legalize Suicide

Being one who entertains in numerous nursing homes, I have the opportunity to observe many elderly citizens who are surviving only because of the application of costly and continuously available medical technology. Many of them also live a miserable existence, during which the financial resources of themselves and their families are gradually exhausted merely in order to prolong life under questionable conditions. From hearing the comments of many of those people, I know that a lot of them resent their current quality of life, and that they would prefer to die if only a legal and painless method of death could be arranged. Methods of bringing about death in a completely painless, comfortable manner are well known to the medical community, but the laws prohibit doctors from causing a patient's death, or even from *assisting* a patient to commit suicide.

One of the characteristics that sets us apart from all other living species is a unique ability to value life. And that is undoubtedly the basis for the laws that prohibit suicide. But, another characteristic that distinguishes us from other living things is the ability to *evaluate* our *quality* of life. We are able to recognize a life that has a high quality, and to distinguish it from one that has a low quality, especially when the latter involves extensive human misery.

There are many human beings who want to preserve *all* human life, regardless of the quality of that life. I happen not to agree with that point of view. I feel that the quality of life should be a significant factor in determining whether human life should be artificially prolonged. There are many cases, of course, in which conditions of misery are only temporary and have a high probability of being reversed. In such cases, we would want to avoid promoting any termination of life. But, in cases in which the miserable conditions of life are irreversible, it seems to me that we should consider permitting the lives of those people who suffer them to be terminated, particularly if they are mentally alert and able to realize the consequences of any decision which they might make about ending their life. It appears to me that legalizing suicide and making painless methods of suicide available to those types of people would be a highly merciful act.

People who promote the idea of prolonging life under even miserable, irreversible, and obviously terminal conditions are doing a disservice to our species, because we are not only capable of appreciating a high quality of life more than any other species, but we also can be more painfully aware of a low quality of life than any other species. I find it hard to believe that anyone who has personally experienced extensive pain and misery themselves could deny the pain-wracked, terminally ill person the right to end a life of misery.

Time To Teach

For several years, I was employed as the Science Coordinator for my school district. In that capacity, I was expected to coordinate the science program for 32 elementary, junior high and senior high schools. It turned out that the factor of time was the greatest barrier to establishing a well-defined scope and sequence for science. It was quite easy to establish one on paper. However, when it came to implementing the program, teachers at the elementary level complained that they didn't have enough time to cover all of the concepts that were listed. This complaint didn't emanate as strongly from the secondary teachers of science, who taught specific courses having designated instructional time.

One solution for the time dilemma at the elementary level would have been to eliminate some of the concepts from the list to be covered. Another would have been to arrange for more time to teach the listed concepts. Neither of those solutions turned out to be acceptable to an identifiable majority of the elementary teachers, however. First of all, none of the aggressive advocates of science at the elementary level was willing to eliminate any concepts from the recommended list. And, in regard to available instructional time at that level, it initially appeared that there was no time problem, because there were no rigid time requirements for any other subjects that could limit the amount of time spent on science. Supposedly, all that the science committee had to do was to issue the scope and sequence for the elementary science program at each grade level to all of the teachers of the respective level, and to tell them that they were expected to cover the concepts listed in the scope and sequence. However, it turned out that there *was* a time problem at the elementary level, because there were approximately thirteen other subjects besides science that every elementary teacher was supposed to cover. An estimate of the time that would be realistically required to teach all of the recommended topics in all of those subjects indicated that the school day would have to be extended from the existing six hours to approximately ten hours. The curriculum guides suggested the need to teach much more than there was time to teach. That problem was exacerbated by the fact that there were fourteen different coordinators for the fourteen different subjects, and each one was applying pressure to the elementary teachers to teach everything that was in their respective guide.

As far as I know, time-allocation problems of the type that existed when I was a coordinator in 1974 still exist in most school districts at the elementary level. I assume that they may be even worse now, because many new topics have been forced upon the elementary level by pressure groups. If that is true, we should take steps to alleviate the almost certain frustration that the situation creates for elementary teachers.

The Advantages Of A Universal Language

A mong sociologists, there is a commonly held belief that the ability of various ethnic groups to communicate effectively between each other leads to better cooperation between them and greatly decreases the probability of conflicts between them. Because *language* is important to communication, it is vital that various groups of people in the world be able to understand each other's language if we can ever have any hope of world harmony.

One method of increasing the understanding of foreign languages is to promote a study of those languages in all countries of the world. However, it is highly unlikely that every group of people who speak a specific native language would ever gain a significant level of knowledge of very many of the other languages. A more realistic approach might be for the leading nations of the world to adopt a policy of promoting a "universal" language. By definition, that would be a language which all nations of the world would encourage their citizens to study as their top priority second language. It would also be the language in which most documents of international communications and trade negotiations would be written. If the most influential nations in the world would adopt such a policy, it seems likely that eventually the other countries would adopt a similar policy in order to maximize the probability that their citizens would be capable of competing in world markets by being able to communicate effectively with all people of all ethnic groups and cultures.

If the leading nations of the world could agree to identify a universal language, the next step would be to decide which language that would be. It would be natural for most countries to want the universal language to be the one that is already their indigenous language. That would make the adoption of the universal language much easier for them, respectively. However, I suspect that the world's renowned linguists would have little difficulty in identifying the *best* language to be used as a universal one. One criterion for deciding would be the ease with which a non-native could learn the language. Another would be the total expressiveness of the language; we would undoubtedly want to use a language that could effectively be used to express the widest possible range of thoughts and ideas. It is a well accepted fact that some languages permit only a limited range of expression, and it is theorized that such limitations of language have corresponding limitations on the thought processes of the people speaking only those languages.

Imagine the increase in understanding between people of various cultures if those people could speak a common language, which they could then use to express clearly their thoughts to each other. We might even hope for a significant reduction in conflicts in the world if such a situation were ever to develop.

Unexpected Bills And Income

Did you ever notice that you frequently get unexpected bills in the mail, but that you hardly ever receive unexpected income? The bills that I'm talking about are those like the one for the new federal boat tax that was passed as a fine-print amendment to a bill to aid small businesses, or a supplementary tax added to this summer's water bill to help to pay for the removal of last winter's unusually large snowfall. What does last winter's snowfall have to do with this summer's water costs, except that there ought to be a lot more water around the county, and the water costs should go down, not up.

If you're a homeowner, there's a significantly increased chance that you will receive a lot of unexpected bills. Most of us who ever bought a brand new home erroneously assumed that nothing would ever wear out or deteriorate. Actually, one can safely assume that anything that has moving parts will eventually break down, and any part of the house that is composed of one or more of the known elements will deteriorate. And did you ever notice how warranted things wear out shortly after the warranty has expired? I found that to be especially true of car batteries. I don't think I ever had a 3-year battery that didn't give out in the 37th month. One unexpected expense that my family had came in a pair. Our clothes washer and clothes dryer broke down within the same week, just as though they were programmed to do that. The

174

breakdown occurred, naturally, shortly after the warranty had expired.

Unexpected income is much harder to come by. My own greatest source of unexpected income comes in the form of an occasional dividend check from my Korea War-era life insurance policy. When I purchased it, it was explained to be a non-participatory policy, with no hope of any kind of dividends. However, the government officials who set up that insurance program must have made some drastic error in planning, because the insurance fund actually makes money each year, and manages to send me a sizeable dividend every now and then.

Most of us receive a lot of potential unexpected income which comes in the mail almost daily in the form of various checks and certificates with numerous strings attached. One of the most frequent types lately has been the check which I simply have to endorse in order to cash it, but the fine print says that by endorsing it I am signing up for some long-term, very expensive service. The most obvious sources of potential unexpected income are those which announce in bold letters on the front of the envelope that I will be awarded several million dollars. Always, however, the bold letters on the front are accompanied by very fine print that begins with the word "if". Of course, even this cynical soul holds out hope that some day he'll receive such a notice with no "if" attached.

Unwanted Babies

I contend that giving birth to an unwanted baby is one of the world's greatest sins. That sin is compounded frequently by mothers who actually end up murdering their newborns. We read about such incidents frequently in reports such as those about dead babies being found wrapped in plastic bags in dumpsters. The world is quick to decry such an act, but you hardly ever hear anyone condemn giving birth to an unwanted baby, who may very well continue life for years in that same unwanted mode. Scientific studies of child development and child-rearing practices have shown that people are more likely to reach their full potential for physical, emotional and social development if they have received an appropriate amount of nurturing during their early years. By "nurturing," I don't mean only the instinctive maternal coddling that is most likely to be administered by the majority of mothers. I also mean the assistance in skill development and knowledge attainment, and frequent expression of the kind of love that goes beyond the instinctive level.

The birth of an unwanted baby who continues on as an unwanted infant, toddler, and adolescent condemns that child almost certainly to a second-class position in society and to a relatively unhappy life. It is extremely unfortunate that the desirability of policies to prevent the birth of unwanted babies isn't given at least as much attention as abortion gets. That

176

fairly common practice is condemned by a significant portion of the human population. Cries of shock, disgust, and anger are routinely expressed as a result of disclosure about abortions that have occurred. And there are, of course, some highly organized large groups that aggressively pursue the opposition to abortion as their primary focus. However, when we compare the seriousness of the two crimes of abortion and giving birth to unwanted babies, I'm not sure which is more grave.

Of course, a way out of this dilemma is to implement methods other than abortion for preventing the birth of unwanted babies. Many of the abortion opponents with whom I speak refer to adoption as being a major answer, but I'm confident that if you compared the numbers of all of the unwanted babies in the world with the numbers of qualified adults wanting to adopt babies, the latter number would seem minuscule.

Because most of the pro-life segment of the population considers the beginning of human life to be the point at which conception occurs, and because those same people interpret any interference with the survival of the organism beyond that point to be abortion, it might be advisable to develop and expand birth control methods *preventing* conception. Furthermore, it might be prudent to make those methods available to *all* potential mothers, free of charge. It seems undeniable that such an approach would reduce significantly the number of births of unwanted babies.

We Need An Educational Voucher System

I would like to propose an alternative to the currently existing public school financial arrangement. I have entitled it the Public Education Voucher System (PEV System or PEVS). Under the provisions of the PEV System, the parents of a school-aged child would be given annually a voucher which could be used at any PEVS school. A critical characteristic of the PEVS school is that it would have to function under the same constitutional constraints under which public schools now have to operate. For example, it could not include religious activities of any type; nor could it practice discrimination in any form. PEVS schools would also have to operate within the limits of state laws and the guidelines established by the State Board of Education, just as schools now do.

The Public Education Voucher (PEV) for each child would have a dollar value which had been predetermined, by the State Board of Education or its assigned representative, for the geographical area in which the child resided. A PEVS student could enroll at any PEVS school within his or her geographical area as long as it included his or her appropriate grade level or achievement level. Upon enrolling the student at the school of his or her choice, the parent would relinquish the voucher, which would subsequently be redeemed by that school for dollars to be added to its operating fund.

The staff of the PEVS school would have a relatively high degree of autonomy in determining instructional methods, selecting instructional materials, and developing instructional programs, within the limits established by federal law, state law, guidelines established by the State Board of Education, and guidelines established by the directors of the school district. Because the amount of funds available to the school would be determined by the number of students it could attract, there is a relatively high probability that the staff would be very responsive to the needs and interests of the potential clientele: the students and their parents.

PEVS schools would be accredited on the basis of a required minimum of instruction in state-designated subjects. Additional instruction should be permitted in other, approved subjects to the degree that the individual school could provide it within the limits of the voucher funds that were available.

Some private schools which are not now constitutionally acceptable as PEVS schools because of religious activities or discriminatory practices might be inclined to forego those activities or practices in order to qualify for the PEVS vouchers. However, any PEVS school, including a former private school, would be free to place major emphasis on special aspects, including, but not limited to discipline, rigor of program, or ethics instruction, as long as those aspects did not constitutionally disqualify it from receiving public funding.

Waste Disposal

The disposal of human-produced waste mate-rials has drawn a lot of fire lately. The NIMBYs (Not In My Back Yard) have been out in force to oppose various forms and locations of waste disposal, especially the disposal of solid wastes in garbage dumps. Those dumps probably rank only second, just behind jails, in attracting the attention of the NIMBYs, who usually don't deny the necessity for such facili-ties; they simply don't want them to be built in their *own* localities.

There may be a simple solution to the waste dis-posal dilemma. Maybe we should pass a law that says that all governmental jurisdictions must arrange for their citizens' waste materials to be disposed of within their own boundaries. The intent of such a law would be to prevent, for example, channeling of sewage or shipping of garbage to other cities, counties, or states. It would certainly reduce the target area of the NIMBYs. They would no longer have to expend the major por-tion of their energies opposing the disposal of wastes of some other jurisdiction, but would, instead, be able to concentrate on the problems created by the need for the disposal of wastes produced by themselves and their own neighbors.

If governmental entities could no longer arrange for the transfer of their wastes to other locations, imagine the rapid increase in public awareness of the environmental impact of such wastes. Currently, many governments are evading that impact by shipping those wastes to some other jurisdiction. For example, cities are notorious for trucking their garbage to some unincorporated area where there is less voter power to resist the garbage dumps where it is deposited. Also, one of the most common practices ever instituted by cities is to channel their *sewage* to the nearest ocean or stream, which, it is assumed, will carry it to away from population centers. The trouble is, the whole earth is rapidly becoming one giant population center.

One benefit of the law which I am suggesting here would be the tremendous stimulus to the economy. Just imagine the scurrying by multitudes of entrepreneurs to develop the *best* waste disposal methods. Entire new industries would arise, resulting in the creation of thousands of new jobs. It might even happen that up to half of the population could be *employed* in the processes of disposing of the wastes of the *total* population. That is about the size of the work force that *I think* would be required to properly dispose of all of the human-produced wastes.

Of course, one major *disadvantage* of the new law would be that a major focus of NIMBYs would be eliminated, and that could enable them to take on projects that are even more onerous than the opposition to garbage dumps and sewage treatment plants.

Is There Life Elsewhere?

The next time you feel as though you're at the center of the universe, and everything in it revolves around *you*, consider some of the numerical figures that make it highly unlikely that you are anything more than a mere speck in the overall scheme of things. First of all, one astronomer told me that there are estimated to be 10,000,000,000 (that's 10 billion) stars in our galaxy, which is known as the Milky Way Galaxy. Then, there are estimated to be about 100,000,000,000 (that's 100 billion) galaxies in the *visible* universe (that's the part that we are able to detect with our best astronomical instruments). For the sake of argument, we might assume that the average number of planets around each star is about 10. By multiplying the foregoing numbers, we come up with an estimate of about 10,000,000,000,000,000,000,000 (that's ten billion trillion) planets in the visible universe. That's not counting what might exist in the part of the universe which is beyond our detection. For all we know, the universe is limitless, which means for all practical purposes, the number of planets in the universe might be limitless.

However, for the sake of discussion, let me limit the numbers to the planets that are estimated to exist in the *visible* universe. Suppose that the probability that life could evolve on any planet is only one in a trillion. That's a relatively small probability, approaching zero. Nevertheless, if there were ten billion trillion planets in the universe, the probability would be relatively high that life has evolved on ten billion of them. So, what do you think is the probability that life has evolved on at least *one other planet* besides the Earth? It would be extremely high, to say the least, approaching infinitesimally high.

If life exists on any other planets besides the Earth, there is always the chance that it is more intelligent, or at least more knowledgeable than the human race. Perhaps it could know how to use the laws of physics and other natural laws to a much greater degree than we know how to use those laws. It is not even inconceivable that a form of life could exist which understands the laws of physics well enough to have the capability for transportation from one part of the universe to another part instantaneously. If that were the case, then UFO's traveling at high speeds would not seem to be unlikely.

If life that is more intelligent and more knowledgeable than the human race were to exist elsewhere in the universe, and if it could visit our planet anytime it wished to, what significance would that have for our security, our religion and our future?

These are just a few things to contemplate the next time you feel that the universe revolves around yourself.

The Value Of Understanding Statistics

When I was studying in college to become a teacher, one of the courses that I was required to take was entitled "Tests And Measurements." Part of that course involved learning about statistical methods: the procedures for helping to determine the probability of the occurrence of certain events.

Now, most of the students in that class detested it. It was very common to hear one of my classmates remark that that class was the most useless one that they had ever taken. I think that a phenomenon that they were manifesting was that a sizeable proportion of adults prefers not to be swayed by logic, and it can't be denied that the application of statistics represents, to a large degree, the application of logic. Many adults would prefer to make their decisions on the basis of ignorance and emotions rather than knowledge and logic. And since statistics represents the latter two, it proves to be a fairly unpopular form of methodology among people of that type.

One very common application of statistics is the determination of manufacturers' levels of confidence in their products. Another application is that of establishing the predictability of natural events. An understanding of statistics makes it possible for one to have more confidence in such applications. On the other hand, ignorance of statistical methods makes it easier to justify a distrust of them.

Another observation that I have made in regard to statistics is that a lot of people ignore statistical probabilities and instead convince themselves of the likelihood of events that have a relatively low probability of occurring. You'll find such people expending a lot of energy and money on low-probability events like lotteries, slot machines, pull tabs, drawings, and the like.

The use of a knowledge of probability doesn't have to be restricted to the formal application of statistical procedures. It can also be applied in very informal ways to daily life. For example, I don't go fishing unless I feel that the chance of catching a fish is at least 50 percent. It is possible for the alert average fisherman to estimate those odds fairly accurately through casual observations. However, I must admit that I kept accurate records of my fish catches for several years and made a graph of those records each year, before I was confident of being able to pinpoint the 50 percent level with reliability.

There are countless similar ways in which an understanding of statistics can make life more fruitful and less stressful. For that to come about, you need to have confidence in statistics and to conduct your life in a manner that takes wise advantage of the numerous ways in which the odds affect you each day.

The Best Problem Solvers

Although knowledge alone does not make a person a good problem solver, I think that it is safe to say that an abundance of knowledge can help to make a person a *better* problem solver. Despite the fact that the ability to remember information isn't the sole determiner of a person's problem-solving ability, the primary elements of that ability, which are the skills of analyzing information and synthesizing ideas from it, are enhanced by having a wealth of knowledge.

When a person is analyzing information - looking for similarities, differences, and ambiguities - that analysis is facilitated by continuous conscious and subconscious references between the information that they are analyzing and the other information that is stored in their brain. That cross-referencing process is improved by the ready availability of large amounts of other accumulated knowledge with which the current information can be compared.

When a person is synthesizing a new idea on the basis of their analysis of information, there is also that continuous cross-referencing process going on. The possible range of ideas that can be developed from the preceding analysis is enlarged in that way. The more stored knowledge that is available, the greater the possibilities for perceiving routes to logical applications of the new information.

If my foregoing assumptions are correct, then, all

other things being equal, the person with the greater amount of knowledge will be the better problem solver. It would follow, then, that parents who want to help their children to improve their problem-solving abilities could achieve that goal in part by providing the children with frequent and extensive exposure to many sources of accurate information. Thus, the parents who have, in the past, purchased sets of encyclopedias for their children may have indirectly been helping the latter to expand their problem-solving skills.

The reason that I say "indirectly" is that a more direct approach to bringing about improvement in thinking skills would be to provide the children with instruction that is intended to improve their skills in analyzing information and synthesizing ideas from it. One of the best ways of accomplishing that is to place them in programs that actually give them practice in analyzing and synthesizing. Such programs may not be easy to find, since the bulk of instructional programs in our schools emphasize primarily the *acquisition* of information, rather than analysis or synthesis. Programs that emphasize the latter two are those such as *inquiry oriented* math, science, and social studies curricula. But, in conjunction with enrolling children in those types of programs, it would appear to be advantageous to arrange also for their accumulation of extensive amounts of information.

187

Why There Are So
Many Single Mothers

Everywhere I go these days, I see single moms. At least I assume that they are single moms: they are escorting one or more kids, and they don't have rings on their left ring fingers. Not only that, but on TV I constantly hear about all of the single moms who are having such a difficult time supporting their kids. How come there are so many single moms?

Well, the answer is a simple one. Most girl babies inherit the "Mom-gene." That gene causes one to place a much higher priority on mom-hood than on sex after the first baby is borne. It also makes one tolerant of wailing babies, dirty diapers, and runny noses. You may be able to infer here that the mom-gene has a delayed effect. It doesn't kick in until the first pregnancy. Up until that time, sex is fairly important to the female human being.

Most boy babies, on the other hand, inherit the "guy-gene" in the place of the mom-gene. The guy-gene makes a person think primarily of one thing: sex, sex, sex. (Maybe that's three things.) It also has a delayed effect that doesn't kick in until about the age of eleven or twelve. (Physiologists explain it by saying that the male sex hormones start to flow about that age.) The guy-gene also has a macho-effect that makes a person strongly desirous of beating other males at just about anything, including, but not limited to war, football, arm-wrestling, and tiddle-dee-winks.

Now the mom-gene and the guy-gene are directly antagonistic to each other. As soon as the mom-gene rears its ugly head in the female, the guy-gene in the male causes him to see the writing on the wall, and starts him to thinking that maybe there are other females around who don't yet suffer from the mom-gene syndrome, and his eyes start wandering. This tendency is hastened by baby-wails, dirty diapers, and runny noses. Added to that is the fact that the guy-gene makes a man long for the untethered, wide-open spaces of bachelorhood. It also causes the married man to think about how his income is no longer *his.* So, he takes off, despite what the law says, and ignores all pleas to support his progeny, opting instead to follow the instincts that the guy-gene have cursed him with. This leaves the mom to singly support and rear the kids whom she so dearly cherishes in spite of their wails, dirty diapers, and runny noses, all due to the influence of the mom-gene.

Use this form to order additional copies of *Purls of Wisdom*

PURLS OF WISDOM [ISBN # 1-886839-12-3]

Quantity____ @ $7.95   Total _____

Add $2.00 for shipping the first
book, 50¢ each book thereafter.   _____

Washington state residents
add applicable sales tax   _____

Total _____

Send order to:
Fun Ed. Productions
22711-66th Ave. Ct. E., Suite 11
Spanaway, WA 98387

NAME_____

ADDRESS_____

CITY_____

STATE_____ ZIP _____